PUB WA
FOR THE F/

West Sus

PUB WALKS
FOR THE FAMILY

West Sussex

Douglas Lasseter

COUNTRYSIDE BOOKS
NEWBURY, BERKSHIRE

COUNTRYSIDE BOOKS
3 Catherine Road
Newbury, Berkshire

ISBN 1 85306 310 X

Designed by Mon Mohan
Cover illustration by Colin Doggett
Maps by the author
Photographs by the author's wife

Produced through MRM Associates Ltd., Reading
Typeset by Paragon Typesetters, Clwyd
Printed and bound by Woolnough Bookbinders, Wellingborough

Contents

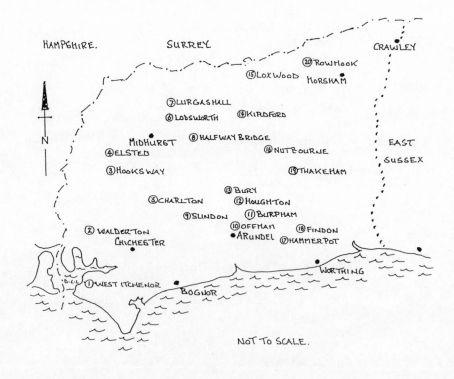

Area map showing locations of the walks.

Introduction

Following my previous book, *Sussex: Walks For Motorists*, I had several appeals, not least from my daughter, for a series of walks which would be within the capability of most families. This would include parents with younger children and those who are not attracted by all-day rambles, or who can no longer undertake such distances. There would also need to be facilities for food and other refreshment.

Allied to these criteria is the desire to protect the British pub and our countryside. I never cease to be amazed at how old this problem is, as illustrated by the following extract from the Sussex poet and author, Hilaire Belloc, who wrote in his collected verse, *This and That* (published in 1912):

> When you have lost your inns
> Drown your empty selves,
> For you will have lost the
> Last of England.

This makes the point for me very well indeed, but pubs, after all, are material things that can be repaired or replaced, which is not the case with our countryside and the wild creatures within it. I take the view that the more of us who get out into the countryside and enjoy it, the bigger the lobby we shall create to protect it. It is heartening to witness the mounting awareness in people of their heritage and the need to maintain it. I hope that this, and similar publications, will go in some small measure towards fostering that awareness.

With these ground rules set, all that remained was for my wife, Eileen, and me, accompanied at times by our young grandson, to record and document these walks, which vary in length from just over 2 miles to the longest of 5¼ miles. All are circular, starting from and returning to the particular pub upon which they are based.

All pubs in this book welcome children and try to foster a family atmosphere. Children under 14 are not allowed in bars by law, but most of the pubs will have some kind of family room and will offer a children's menu, often at reduced prices. In summer, pub gardens come into their own as the best places for families to congregate, and some pubs will provide outdoor play facilities, or maybe a games room, to keep children happy.

It would be reasonable to say that I am biased in my description of the countryside in which these walks are set. It is not usually my custom to use such extravagant expressions as 'spectacular views', but these are exactly the words used by my grandson to describe the scenery laid out before us across the Arun valley as we rested a while in Arundel Park.

In every case, within a few hundred yards of the start of the walks, you will be in a different world. This demands that some simple precautions are taken. Short though these walks may be, it would be extremely unwise to attempt them in flimsy footwear, particularly sandals. Wellingtons are not a good idea either. Good-quality trainers give protection over rough and stony ground, while even better are leather walking boots. Warm garments are important in case the weather turns chilly and can always be removed and carried.

However short the walk, dehydration can be the most common cause of discomfort, particularly on hot days. Drinking fruit juices is fine, but this can make you more thirsty. Water is highly recommended, carried in a cool flask. Most young people have rucksacks for school and these serve equally well for carrying water and surplus garments.

A simple sketch map of the route of each walk accompanies the text. You are recommended to use an Ordnance Survey Landranger or Pathfinder map in conjunction with this, as it will help you get the most from the walk. Sheet numbers of both the 1:50 000 and 1:25 000 scales of map are quoted. Make sure that your position is relative to the various landmarks quoted in each text.

There may be instances where you do not use a particular pub's parking facilities, but park in the village street. In doing so you must ensure that you cause no obstruction. Every landlord of the pubs quoted in this book has been contacted by the author and permisssion to use the various pubs' car parks should be readily given, providing that the pub is patronised before or after the walk. There are two instances, however, where I suggest that you use the alternatives nearby.

Having taken the trouble to read this far, you are well on the way, so get out there with your family into 'your' countryside. But please observe the Country Code. The only things you should leave behind you are your footprints; take all your litter home; close and fasten gates behind you; control the family dog.

None of these walks is qualified with a time in which it can be completed. They will take as long as you want them to. A simple rule of thumb is that you will cover the ground at between 2-2½ miles per hour. I hope you enjoy the walks in this book as much as I have.

Douglas Lasseter
spring 1994

Publisher's Note

We hope that you obtain considerable enjoyment from this book; great care has been taken in its preparation. However, changes of landlord and actual closures are sadly not uncommon. Likewise, although at the time of publication all routes followed public rights of way or well-established permitted paths, diversion orders can be made and permissions withdrawn.

We cannot accept responsibility for any inaccuracies, but we are anxious that all details covering both pubs and walks are kept up to date, and would therefore welcome information from readers which would be relevant to future editions.

To 'Eileen' and Susan and all our loyal friends in
The Sussex Wayfarers walking group, who will understand that:

The great hills of the South Country
They stand along the sea;
And it's there walking in the high woods
That I could wish to be,
And the men that were boys when I was a boy
Walking along with me.

Hilaire Belloc from 'Verses'
written in 1910 on Battersea Bridge

1 West Itchenor
The Ship

The Ship, built in 1935, replaced a much older, 18th century building on the same site.

This large pub, very busy on summer weekends and in the holiday season with 'yachties' and small-boat sailors, is a perfect venue for indulging in seafood, in particular crab, lobster and prawns, all caught locally off Bognor and Selsey. What a feast they make, either with a simple fresh salad or served in many innovative and delicious ways. Although the pub specialises in shellfish, there are plenty of other choices on the bar and restaurant menus. The proprietors, Pam and John, serve children's meals at reduced prices.

Telephone: 0243 512284.

How to get there: West Itchenor is situated about 10 miles south-west of Chichester. Turn south off the A27, take the A286 and continue into the B2179 West Wittering road to the second minor road turning right (north) signposted 'Shipton Green and West Itchenor'.

Parking: Permission to use the pub's car park will be readily granted providing the pub is patronised. There is no street parking in the village. Alternatively, there is a large field car park which is signposted near the pub with hourly or all day charges.

Length of the walk: 3¾ miles. Maps: OS Landranger 197, Pathfinder SU 60/70 and SU 80/90 (inn GR 799013).

Much of this walk is by the sea (Chichester Harbour of course). It is full of variety and interest, having two sections on the harbour shoreline, as well as going over farmland and through woods. As you go down to the Hard, you will see, outside the harbour office, the advertisement for harbour boat trips – it all makes a wonderful day out. On small-boat race days in the summer, one wonders if there could possibly be room on the water for the boat trippers.

One is never far away from the sight of the Downs in Sussex and certainly not here, where there are good views of a considerable stretch of them. This walk is all over flat terrain.

Chichester Harbour, West Itchenor.

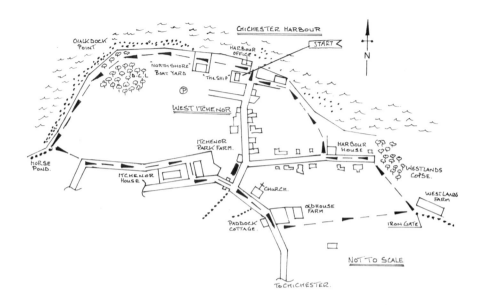

The Walk

From the pub, walk down towards the Hard and, at the harbour office, turn left to follow the way sign into a narrow path. This will come out onto the Hard at Northshore yacht yards. Continue on the footpath opposite and this path, with its metalled surface, will bend round into an area with a seat. Walk ahead on the path, which will follow the shoreline to Chalkdock Point and will then enter an area of woodland. Going over a plank bridge, the path continues, with trees on the right, coming then to a three-way sign at Horse Pond. Turn left, going through a 'squeeze' gate leading onto a field path.

Go over the next stile at a way sign, bearing left onto a farm track and walking towards Itchenor Park Farm. When you reach the farm buildings, turn right over a stile at a two-way sign by a metal gate. With the farm boundary wall on your left, bear left, then right through a gate set in the wall. Walking ahead to the lane junction, turn left and continue through the entrance gates of Itchenor Park and on to the road.

Ensure that you keep to the right-hand side of the road (to face the oncoming traffic). There are places where you can use the grass verge. Pass by St Nicholas' church, a 13th century

13

building which is well worth a visit, then, with Old House Farm on your left followed by Paddock Cottage on the right, turn left across the road. Go over a plank bridge at a way sign and Old House Farm is now immediately on your left.

This short section of path will emerge into a large yard area which contains a single large storage building. With this on your left, walk on to continue on the obvious path across the fields. The buildings of Westlands Farm will come into view. You will arrive at an old iron gate which has a three-way sign behind it. Turn around to have the gate behind you and bear to your right into the other path, heading towards the trees of Westlands Copse, now in front of you. The path will go into the woods and will exit at a way sign. Turn left into the lane, which will continue on for about ¼ mile between large houses.

Coming then to a house called The Anchorage and its neighbour, Harbour House (both on the right), turn right at the way sign into a narrow path, which will lead out onto the harbour path. This will come to a two-way sign at a white painted building. Turn left onto a gravel path leading to a gravel lane at the end of which, on the opposite side of the road, is the Ship.

② Walderton
The Barleymow

The Barleymow was, originally, a pair of cottages, built around 1740 in the isolated farming community of that period. It has, of course, been considerably added to and has retained its charm in the process. Although the deeds have not survived, testaments to its origins are to be seen in the many old photographs and documents on display within the building. In summer it is especially delightful, with hanging flower baskets. Clive Grace, the proprietor, welcomes parents with young children as long as they do not disturb other customers and do not use the bar. There is a children's play area and a secluded garden. The pub has an extensive menu of bar and restaurant food and, in addition, children's portions at adjusted prices are available. Curries are the speciality here, and very popular they are, too.
Telephone: 0705 631321.

How to get there: Walderton is west of Chichester and east of

Rowlands Castle. The village is reached by an unlisted road turning north-east to Stoughton and the Mardens from the B2146 road.

Parking: Permission to use the pub's large car park, while you walk, is readily given, providing the establishment will be patronised. Alternatively, parking space is available at the junction of the B2146 and Stoughton road on the east side of the river Ems road bridge.

Length of the walk: 4¼ miles. Maps: OS Landranger 197, Pathfinder SU 61/71 (inn GR 790106, car park GR 788105).

There is a subtle change in the nature of the countryside in this area, reminiscent of Hampshire, whose eastern border is only a short distance away, and how beautiful it is, with rolling wooded downland, giving views across to Stansted Forest, the Solent and Isle of Wight. This is an easy walk over undulating terrain. Some of the tracks are rough and stony, but always well drained. There is a large population of wild deer around here.

The Walk
From the Barleymow car park, turn right onto the road and walk back to the junction, on the B2146, of the Walderton, West Marden and Compton roads. You will pass by on the right, just before the junction, the parking area at the river Ems road bridge. Cross over the road to continue, with the houses on your left. Where the main road bends, leave it and bear left into the lane. Heacham Cottage will be on your left. Then, with Down Land Cottage on the right, the lane starts to climb gently. After some way and passing a rebuilt flint and brick house on the left and with the woods of Lordington Copse on the same side, continue up the lane to where it bends sharply to the left. Now, with a way sign on your right, leave the lane, walking ahead into the stone track. Shortly beyond, at a three-way sign, bear left at the fork.

The track will start to level out and open ground will be on the left, giving views towards Stansted Forest. The woods of Watergate Hanger will be on your right. Broad Reed Farm will appear across the open ground as will the Old Lodge House which stands beside the track leading to the farm and Stansted

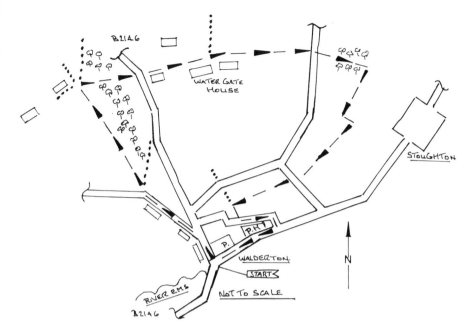

House. On reaching Old Lodge House, bear right, then turn right at a four-way sign into a wide woodland track. Now coming to a two-way fork with a way sign on the left, take the left-hand fork and this will descend steeply – still through woodland – and will bear left at a two-way sign and continue downhill. With a three-way sign on the right and a large house beyond, the path will emerge onto the B2146 road. Cross straight over into Locksash Lane opposite and North Lodge will be on your right.

The lane continues, with Watergate Park on the right, then comes to a junction, the left-hand branch of which goes off to Watergate Farm. Walk straight ahead. Watergate House is on the right. Passing by the two entrance ways to the house and few yards beyond the last one, turn right at the three-way sign into the continuing stone track, where you will shortly pass by a Sussex timber barn on your right, followed by a gate and a two-way sign on the left.

The track will be rising gently now. On your left will be a timber fence, which will eventually give way to an iron one (a relic from Victorian times). Now the track goes into Woodbarn

Woods – the iron fence ends here. The track will again rise. At the top, and coming to a two-way sign on the right, take the right-hand fork of the track, which will shortly bring you to a two-way sign on your left. Bear left. Along the course of this track and looking to the right (south), you will get good views across to the Isle of Wight. The track will start to descend – the woods are still on your left, with open ground on the right. At a two-way sign on your left, the path will go through a narrow section of woods. On reaching a junction of paths at a three-way sign on the left, turn right. This particularly rough and stony path will bring you out onto the Walderton to Upmarden road.

Cross straight over the road. The field path will go by a two-way sign and hedge on the left, which you will follow. The rising path will enter Inholmes Wood, where you will need to watch the tree roots under foot. With a three-way sign on the right, turn right into a large field. Almost immediately you will pass by, on the right, a timber power line support. Having crossed the field, the path continues, with trees on your right. Walderton can now be seen across the fields.

Climb a stile at a two-way sign onto a lane, to turn right and quickly left over another stile onto another field path. A hedge will be on the right. After following the hedge for some way, a two-way sign will direct you through it and over a stile. The hedge will now be on your left and, shortly beyond, at a double power line support with a three-way sign, go over the stile here into a path enclosed by fences. This will take you by houses and out onto the village street at the back of the Barleymow pub. Turn left to continue down to the road, coming out by a telephone box. Turn right to reach the pub and your car a short way beyond. If you have parked at the area of the road junction and bridge, then it is only a short distance past the pub.

Hooksway
The Royal Oak

This is another pub whose origins have been lost – not surprisingly, as the building is known to be 400 years old, built in the last decade of the 16th century. It is likely that it became an alehouse in the 1800s and one of its landlords, Alfred Ainger, with his wife Carrie, must surely hold a near record for long-serving landlords, 1907–1971 (64 years), taking over the ownership from his father. A feature of the pub is its many photographs and a framed newspaper article which concerns itself mainly with Alfred Ainger. The pub has been extended but not destroyed. The old 'Four Ale' bar still has its brick floor. The present owners, David and Sarah Jeffery, are keen to encourage parents with young families and offer, in addition to their extensive restaurant and bar food menus, a range of children's meals at very reduced prices. There is a large garden with a play area for children. Summertime brings live band nights and barbecues, both held in the open and very popular.
   Telephone: 0243 59257.

How to get there: Hooksway lies between South Harting and Chilgrove on the B2141 road, south-east of Petersfield. The signposted lane, which is a cul-de-sac to the hamlet and pub, turns east off the main road. Going into and out of the lane you must be ready to use the passing places along its narrow length.

Parking: There is a large adjoining car park which the landlord is happy for walkers to use, with the usual proviso that the pub is patronised either before or after the walk. You should note that it is not possible to park in the adjacent farm tracks and offending vehicles will be towed away!

Length of the walk: 3 miles. Maps: OS Landranger 197, Pathfinder SU 81/91 (inn GR 816162).

This walk is in beautiful hill country with magnificent views. The track you will use on leaving the pub is about ¾ mile long and climbs quite gently to 247 ft in that distance (like Everest it also has a downside!). It then meets the junction of the South Downs Way and you are directed a short way beyond to the Devils Jumps – five Bronze Age burial chambers and a place of much interest for you to visit. On the return route, you will pass by the memorial to Hauptman Joseph Oestermann, 1915–1940. Also on the return leg, you will get a good view of Telegraph House to the west across the valley.

The Walk
Leave the pub car park and turn left onto the farm track. On your left will be the Hide-Away Restaurant and on the right a large house. Almost immediately, you will be in an area which has three tracks leading away from it, left and right. You continue ahead into the middle of the three, which is a wide, rising, stone track. At this junction there is a two-way sign on your right, indicating the path going off in that direction through a gateway. The track will pass by, on both sides, areas of woodland and open ground.

At the bottom of this track you may have seen a notice which read 'West Dean Estates: These Stacks Are Dangerous. Please Keep Off'. You will now encounter another such notice, the significance of which is now apparent. They refer to large stacks of cut timber which are unstable. Just beyond the stacks, make a fork and continue into the left-hand one. Further on you may

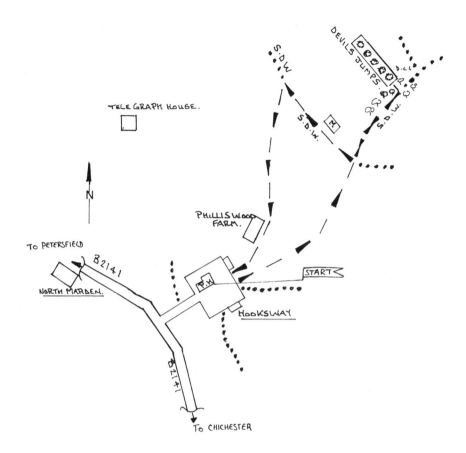

pause to take a breather. Turn around and look south across the Downs to the Solent and Isle of Wight. From some distance away you will have seen your next landmark, the four-way sign at the junction of this track with the South Downs Way. On reaching it, continue straight ahead into the east-bound track of the South Downs Way, making your way now towards the site of the Devils Jumps, only a short distance ahead. The area containing this ancient site is not signposted or advertised in any way, to encourage only the determined, so you will need to keep a sharp look-out for the entrance path. Once beyond the four-way sign, you will again have woods on either hand. As you proceed you will see ahead of you an area of open

21

Memorial stone, Hooksway.

ground on the left as the South Downs Way continues. Here, also on your left, is a well concealed path. Turn into it and, in a few yards, you can read about this site from the notice-board displayed by The Society of Sussex Downsmen.

When you are ready, return to the South Downs Way – turning right, back to the four-way sign. There, turn right again and you are now on the west-bound path of the South Downs Way. In a very short while Hauptman Joseph Oestermann's memorial cairn will be on your right. This German bomber pilot, returning from a raid on Aldershot in 1940 in a Heinkel III, was shot down. Ensuring that his crew could escape safely, he remained with his aircraft which crashed nearby. His body was never recovered. As you continue along the track you will get a wonderful view of Beacon Hill (796 ft) directly ahead of you. Then, with a West Dean gate and fence on your right, you will pass a track going off to the left. You, however, still continue straight ahead and then, with a three-way sign on your left, bear left into a grassy track. From this point, you will already be able to see another three-way sign. Turn sharply left when you reach it and, leaving the South Downs Way, you will be reversing your direction and going gently uphill. You will come to a track going to your left (which you should recognise as you passed by its other end a short time ago). There will be, just beyond this, a two-way sign on your right. Here is a good place to get a view of Telegraph House across the valley. This is one of a long chain of Telegraph Houses stretching from Portsmouth to Admiralty Arch in London. These were Naval Semaphore Stations for relaying messages to Their Lordships in Whitehall. Almost unbelievably, in 1805 the message advising the arrival of Admiral Nelson's body at Portsmouth took only 19 minutes to transmit. One can assume it was good visibility on that day!

From this point, it is now truly downhill all the way back. This track will come out into a clearing and you bear right out of it and, almost immediately, the buildings of Phillis Wood Farm will be in front of you. As well as this farm, there is a Phillis Wood, Phillis Wood Down, Phillis Wood Lane.

Going through a gateway across the track at the farm (now a private residence), you will be approaching the other buildings comprising Hooksway, then shortly getting another, rather pleasant, view of the Royal Oak pub.

Elsted
The Three Horseshoes

Elsted and district enjoys, even in this mad and mindless age, a refreshing air of rural peace. This is so with its dear old pub, which is totally unspoilt. The exterior of the building belies its interior, which as soon as you step over its threshold takes you into a bygone age. It requires very little imagination to transport yourself back to those quieter times. The pub formed part of a complex, built in 1540, which comprised the village stores and butcher's shop. The area which housed the latter survives and is still used, being the room at the lower level and to the right of the bar as you go in. It is believed that the pub started life with its present day name, in itself unusual. Of special significance to me is that the Three Horseshoes was used by Hilaire Belloc, our Sussex poet and author, as his penultimate stopping place with his three companions on their journey on foot in 1902 from Robertsbridge to South Harting, the events of which he used as material for his book *The Four Men*.

There are two areas within the pub available to parents with children and, although the owners, Andrew and Susan Beavis, have no special children's menus, they will gladly supply extra plates so that meals can be shared. All the food is prepared from fresh produce, cooked on the premises, and is predominantly English country fare. There is a huge garden, with a population of cheeky Bantam cocks and hens – a marvel that they survive the local foxes. The beautiful backdrop of the South Downs makes this a relaxed, almost picnic-like venue for a summer salad meal.

Telephone: 0730 825746.

How to get there: Elsted is approximately 2 miles east of South Harting and 4 miles west of Cocking. Using the B2141 road, turn east at South Harting. From the A286 road, turn west at Cocking, then continue via Bepton and Treyford, but this narrow country road must be negotiated with caution. There is access also by turning south off the A272 at Stedham then continuing via Lower Elsted.

Parking: The car park is signposted off the village lane and is opposite the village hall. There is no problem in using the large area while you walk, and permission to do so will be readily given to customers.

Length of the walk: 3¾ miles. Maps: OS Landranger 197, Pathfinder SU 81/91 (inn GR 818196).

The walk, which is over beautiful rolling farmland, is bounded by the nearby South Downs and the more distant hills to the north, giving marvellous views in both directions. An interesting feature of the walk is that it actually goes through two farms, one of which involves a climb over a stockyard gate. The route continues on to the hamlet of Treyford where the houses are built mainly of a particular type of hard chalk, obtained locally, which gives them a warm mellow glow.

The Walk
From the car park, go back out onto the village street and turn right. Then, with the north aspect of the pub on your right, bear right up the sloping roadway leading to the front of the pub and the parking area for Hillview Cottage. You will pass a way sign

on the left on the slope. Bearing slightly right and in a few yards coming to a two-way sign on the right, go down the concrete path with a metal hand rail on the right. You will now be going down the garden path of No 7 – the house on your right. Walk on down the path, passing a way sign and other buildings on your left. Turn right over a stile at a three-way sign, taking you into a field, on the other side of which you will see the next way sign in front of you.

Once there, go through the hedge and bear left into a narrow field. Coming to a hedge on the other side, turn right and the field path continues, with the hedge on your left. At the next two-way sign, turn left over the stile, going over a plank bridge to bear right and on to the next stile and way sign. Go over this stile and the one immediately opposite a few yards away, and you will be on a broad grass track in a field which is usually cultivated. As you walk on up the rising ground the roof of your next landmark, a house called Grevatts, will appear. The grass track will take you straight to a metal gate and two-way sign. Go over the stile here and turn right onto the metalled lane. The house is now in full view. Almost immediately, turn left into a farm track. A way sign and notice-board for New House Farm will be on the right, Grevatts, of course, is on the left. Next to appear (on the left) will be a pair of estate houses, with the farm now well in sight beyond. Then, passing a four-way sign on the right, carry on to the farm. With the farmhouse now on your left, the concrete roadway bears off to the right, leading straight into the stockyards, where you will probably find the gates wired or lashed together. You will have to climb over – on no account should you release them. Needless to say, any dog with you should be on a lead here.

Leaving the stockyards and buildings and coming to a two-way sign on the left shortly beyond them, turn left. Then, bearing right, walk on to a gate in the corner of the small field. At the two-way sign, go over the stile and turn right. There will be a hedge on your right, at the end of which turn right over a stile at a two-way sign. Walk across the short stretch of field to its opposite neighbour, going over this stile. I have to warn you that the fingerboard of the way sign here may be pointing in the wrong direction. You must bear away to the right across this field and be heading towards a group of six oak trees and

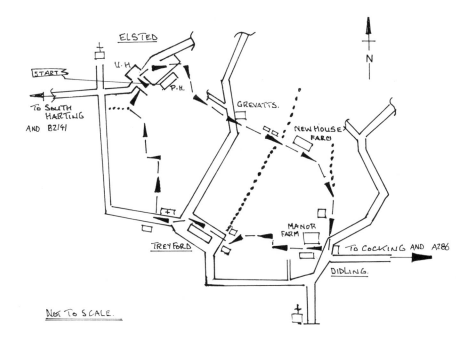

a hedge. When you reach the trees you will find the two-way sign and stile which takes you into the field beyond. You may also find this cultivated and the short distance of footpath may not have been reinstated. If this is the case, simply walk around the field headland to get to the gate and way sign which you can see. You will also see the farm buildings of Didling Manor Farm away to your right. Once over the gate, go over a plank bridge and walk up the rising ground in front of you. There is no perceptible path in the turf. However, keeping a solitary tree on the rising ground to your left and getting to the top, walk on towards the hedge and fence now in front of you. You will very shortly see a three-way sign and stile – go over it and turn right. This path will take you down to the houses in front of you – the village of Didling. Go by a gate across the track, a way sign will be on the right. In only a short way you will join the entrance drive to Old Cottage. Turn left and walk down to the road. With a way sign on the right, turn right.

Almost immediately you will pass by Didling Manor, on your right. Then, only a short way further on and with a way sign on

27

the left, turn right into the barn and stockyards of Didling Manor Farm. On a wide concrete roadway now, with the farm buildings on the right, walk straight ahead to a fence. Beyond this as you get nearer, a short way out into the field, is your next way sign. First, you will have to go through a gate, which you may not recognise as such – a collapsible one, operated by a lever. Watch out for your fingers when you operate this contraption. Once beyond the gate, walk over to the way sign and, with it on your right, continue down the field in the direction of the way sign finger. This will take you down into the corner of the same field and there, at another two-way sign, you must negotiate a second collapsible gate. Now in another field, with a hedge and trees on your right, walk on up this path. At the other end of the field, with a two-way sign in the corner, turn left. Very shortly go right at another two-way sign over two stiles. Still with a hedge on the right, continue on the field path. On your left will be a good view of Beacon Hill with the South Downs Way climbing up its north face. Coming to the end of this field, at a way sign, turn right, then immediately left over a stile to bring the hedge on the left.

At the next two-way sign, go over the stile. Here you need to take care – the path descends quite steeply for a short way. At the bottom, go over the stile there, crossing a pretty brook. A two-way sign will be on the right. Now you are on a wide grassy track which goes through a small pleasant wooded area. The track comes out between two houses (both built with the local hard chalk) onto the lane opposite a way sign – turn right. Just beyond the houses you pass, on the right, a way sign at a flight of steps which is set in the side of the bank. Walk on to the lane junction and, with a house on the left called Rubbin Cottage, turn right. Very soon, on the right, you will pass by an area in the bank of exposed stratified chalk – the material used for much local building. Coming then to a T-junction, turn left into the lane signposted 'Elsted and Harting'. Another house will appear in front of you, but before you reach it, you will pass by an old cemetery on the right, which is now designated as a conservation area – the notice-board will give you the details.

As you come to Treyford Cottage, turn right off the lane at the way sign. Here you should note that the right of way follows the field path with a hedge on your left – not the wide farm track which runs parallel to it on the left. Walk towards the two-way sign and stile, which is on the left (by an old gnarled oak tree) and go across the field, with a hedge on the left. Go over two stiles with a bridge between. Now follow the field path to its corner, turning right there at the two-way sign. Turning left over the next stile at a two-way sign (with a hedge on the right), follow the field path as it descends down to a substantial wooden bridge. From here the path climbs up into the next field, with the hedge still on your right.

Very shortly, reaching a three-way sign, turn right over a stile and, crossing a small field, go over another stile which will take you into a pleasant enclosed path. With a two-way sign on the left, go through a small wicket gate which is opposite. Please ensure that you secure this gate behind you. This brings you into the garden of the bungalow now on your left. A series of paving stones have been set in the grass. Having reached the other side of this garden, you will be back in the pub's car park, having climbed the last stile!

5 Charlton
The Fox Goes Free

This delightful old, unspoilt inn, built around 1540, would have started life as part of a farm complex. Its last function prior to becoming a pub was as the district bakery, the evidence of which is still to be seen. It was first called the Pig and Whistle, then renamed the Fox, and in 1988 was bought from the brewery by its current owner, Gil Battley, who changed the name again, this time with a cunning twist which is not readily apparent. The area generally, and Charlton in particular, has long been associated with hunting and within that fraternity Gil Battley has many associations and, as many of us these days prefer that the fox should go free, so does Mr Battley. However, the change of name was a sly dig, the fox was actually freed from the brewery! Interestingly, this pub, on November 9th, 1915, was the meeting place in which the foundation for the W.I. (Women's Institute) organisation within England was laid. A plaque commemorating this event is displayed in one of the bars. Very unusually, Gil Battley has, in partnership, another

Fox Goes Free, but in France, Lemas du Renard at Bagard, deep in the French countryside near Montpellier and Avignon. All fresh produce is used in the preparation of the wide range of the Fox's restaurant menus. The choice of bar food is also extensive, including several kinds of soup. There is a children's menu and room and a large, pleasant garden looking out onto open countryside.
Telephone: 0243 811461.

How to get there: Charlton lies approximately 6 miles north-east from the centre of Chichester (or 1 mile north from Goodwood racecourse) and can be reached by turning east off the A286, Chichester to Haslemere road, at Singleton or by turning west off the A285, Chichester to Petworth road, at Upwaltham. This latter road, via Droke and East Dean, must be negotiated with caution.

Parking: Specific parking space for the pub is very restricted. We suggest that as there are adequate alternatives, you should either use the lane opposite the pub on grass verges by the public telephone box, or park in North Lane just a little way beyond the pub to the west.

Length of the walk: 2¾ miles. Maps: OS Landranger 197, Pathfinder SU 81/91 (inn GR 889130).

You start by contouring around Levin Down, which is managed by the Sussex Wild Life Trust. You will be totally surrounded by hills and views on this walk – even as you descend to the village of Singleton, one of the jewels of our Sussex villages, with its many old thatched buildings, two pubs and much photographed village pond. The route will take you through part of the village and up to the parish church which is built on Saxon foundations, the nave walls are also Saxon as are some of the doorways – the old building is well worth a visit. Leaving the church, your direction will turn to the east via the field paths back to Charlton.

The Weald and Downland Open Air Museum is close by, with Goodwood racecourse only a mile away (not forgetting Goodwood House, of course).

The Walk
Assuming that you have parked in the lane opposite the pub,

31

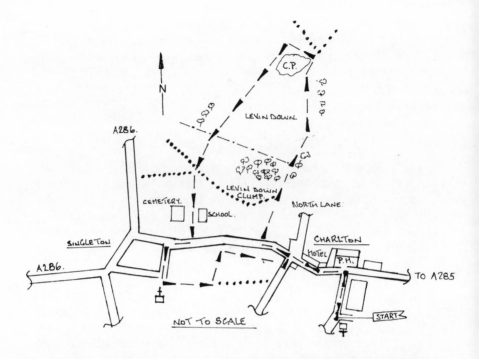

walk back to the road and turn left. If you have parked in North Lane, simply pick up the directions from the lane and road junction. With the pub on the right, walk on past the Woodstock House Hotel on the same side and, just beyond North Lane and Corner Cottage, walk straight on. Then, at the Charlton village boundary marker, turn right off the road, going over a stile at a way sign into a field. Ahead of you, at the foot of the trees, will be your next landmark – a stile, which when you reach it will be a double one with approach steps and a three-way sign. Go over these, turning into the right-hand fork of the two paths. At this spot will be the first of two Sussex Wild Life Trust notice-boards. This is a Site of Special Scientific Interest and, in season, it abounds with many varieties of wild orchid and other wild flowers (forgive me if I remind you here that it is illegal to pick wild flowers). Now, with trees on the right, you will very soon come to a gateway at a two-way sign and in only a few yards the public right of way bears to the left. You continue into this – do not be deceived into continuing on the path with the

32

trees close by on your right. The path continues up along the shoulder of the hill on the open downside.

Coming to a fence across the path, go over the stile and continue on beyond. Then, after some way, you will reach another Sussex Trust information board at a two-way sign. Walk on and shortly the path becomes enclosed by woods on either side. Next, go over a stile set in a fence at a two-way sign and turn right. You are now out on Levin Down. Keeping the fence close by on your right, walk on to the trees ahead of you and, coming to another fence, go over the stile at a two-way sign. Go through a narrow section of trees then, at a three-way sign, go down a flight of steps onto a wide chalky farm track. Bear left at this point and you will pass by the entrance of an old disused chalk pit. Continue to bear left, still on the farm track, and very shortly there will be a four-way sign on your right. Walk over to a three-way sign at a wicket gate. Also on the right at this point, is a tall post with various dates ascribed to the Charlton Hunt.

Go through a metal gate set across the track. Please note that you are obliged, as directed by notices, to leash and restrain dogs in this area. Please also close this gate behind you. The second notice denotes a boundary.

You are now on the open expanse of the top of Levin Down. Follow the vehicle tracks in the turf, leading away from the last gate, and you should endeavour to walk straight ahead. Continue for some considerable way, keeping trees just in sight over to your right. Then, as you top the rising ground, the trees of Levin Clump will start to appear to the left of front. With three isolated trees close by on your right and Levin Clump in clear view on the left, you will see a gate set in a fence at a two-way sign ahead of you. (You should note that, if you have wandered off course to either left or right, you will be confronted by this fence across the Down – simply follow the fence one way or the other and you will come to this gate and way sign.) Go through the gate, ensuring once again please that you secure it behind you and your dog remains leashed. Leading away from this gate is an unmistakable track which very soon will follow the perimeter of a deep depression in the downside to your right. Then, coming to a four-way sign on your left, continue on beyond it. Only a short way further on,

Water lifting windmill at the Weald and Downland Open Air Museum, at nearby Singleton. The museum will appeal to all ages and is well worth a visit.

34

and with the sunken track going towards a gate in front of you, turn left at a three-way sign on that side. Then, bearing right towards a line of trees, you will see a stile which, when you get to it, will be a double one at a two-way sign. Once over this obstacle, you will see Singleton village laid out below. Follow the clear path down to a hedge and, with this on your right and passing a little cemetery on the same side, and then with the school on your left, go out onto the road and turn right.

At a road junction, walk straight ahead – Croft Cottage will be on your left. Then, at the next forking junction, with The Old School on your left, take the left fork. You will immediately see the church and its entrance gate ahead of you. Walk up to it. The route continues by turning left, only a few feet before reaching the church gate. Obviously if, as I hope, you visit this lovely old building, then turn right when you leave it. You will come out into the parking area of some apartments – simply walk ahead between the houses to come out onto a road. Go across it into the continuing path where there is a way sign on your right. Continuing between tall yew hedges, the path bends around to come to a wicket gate at a way sign. This takes you out onto a field path where the buildings of Charlton are ahead of you across the fields. Continue, with horse paddocks on your left, and, coming to the end of these, either go straight across the fields (if the path has been reinstated after seeding) or (if it has not) then simply follow the grassy farm track around the field headland which will bring you to two gates, either of which you can use, taking you out onto the lane.

As you approach these gates you will also see, to your right, the way sign and stile which normally you would have gone over, this also leads onto the lane. Whichever method you choose, turn left onto the lane, which will bring you to the road junction. Opposite is North Lane with Corner Cottage on your right.

Your directions are now determined by where you left your car.

6 Lodsworth
The Hollist Arms

This quaint old pub has the unique feature of a mature red chestnut tree surrounded by a seat outside its front door. A building has existed on this same site since 1401 and it is believed that the pub, much as it is seen in the present day, took its name in the late 1700s from the local family, Hollist, still resident in the village. The family crest is displayed on the pub sign.

English country game is predominant on the menu at this delightful house, but there is also a very wide range of other food available, all cooked to order, using fresh ingredients. The pub has a quiet, secluded garden – the very place in which to enjoy a summer salad meal, of local produce. Nicholas Kennard, joint partner at the Hollist, is justifiably proud of this delightful house and makes provision for family groups.

Telephone: 079 85 310.

How to get there: Lodsworth is situated 1½ miles north of the A272 road, approximately midway between Midhurst and Petworth.

Parking: The Hollist has a car park just north of the pub itself, which the landlord is happy for walkers to use, providing they seek his permission and patronise the pub.

Length of the walk: 4¼ miles. Maps: OS Landranger 197, Pathfinder SU 82/92 (inn GR 928231).

The walk is over magnificent, undulating countryside giving wonderful views, going through woods and across farmland. There is one steep section of Hoe Hill to climb, but it is short, being only about 400 yards long. What a delight this unspoilt village is, as you will see for yourself. You will pass close to the parish church of St Peter. This church, and especially its churchyard, are well worth a short diversion to visit. The churchyard has many magnificent trees (to arboretum specimen standard), including a huge Chilean pine (Araucaria Araucana, monkey puzzle). The resident yew tree is a mere youngster, compared to others in the country, being only an estimated 1,200 years old!

The Walk

From the pub, take the lane signposted 'Sports Ground' (on the green at the chestnut tree). This will take you past the junction of School Lane on the right, and the sports ground further on. Coming to Heathend Farm on the right, bear right into the way-marked 'woodland path'. This will lead to a three-way sign. Turn right. This deeply water-worn path will climb gently, between trees. Eventually, the buildings of Vining Farm will appear on the left.

With a three-way sign to the front, walk on towards a main grid pylon, first passing by another way sign on the right. Just before coming to the power pylon at a four-way sign, walk on to a ruined gateway – the pylon will still be on your left. This wide track will continue downhill. In the valley bottom, turn right through a gate, with a way sign on the right.

You are now at the bottom of Hoe Hill and will pass by another way sign on this steep, but short, climb. On reaching the top, pass on the right another two-way sign. Continue on this flat woodland path to the next three-way sign and turn right. This descending track will bring you to a gate at a two-way sign and out into an open field. Here the path continues, with the woods of Snapelands Copse on the left. Go through

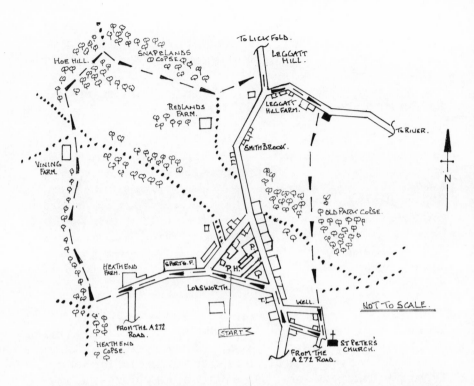

two more gates onto a farm track. Just before reaching Redlands
Farm, turn left over a stile at a three-way sign into a field.

Keep the trees close by on your left and you will now be
walking parallel to the power lines on your left. This will bring
you to a gate, stile and way sign in the corner of the field. Go
over the stile and walk on the short way to the Lickfold road
and turn right, then left into the lane signposted 'Leggatt Hill'.
There will be buildings on your right, Little Leggatt Hill and
Keets. Just beyond, turn right into the yard of Leggatt Hill Farm
through the entrance gates. There is a way sign on the other side
of the road. Go through another gate then, just beyond, with a
gate and track on the left. Walk on into the wide grassy farm
track ahead with hedge and trees on the right.

The track continues through a metal gate into a field. Follow
the vehicle tracks along by a hedge on the right towards the
woods of Old Park Copse. Coming to a metal gate and way sign,
go over the stile. The path, now going through the woods, will

38

The ancient well of St Peter, Lodsworth.

come to a three-way sign on the left. Bear left, still on the woodland path. Next, going over a stream, go through a gate with a three-way sign on the right and walk straight ahead into a field. Again, clear vehicle tracks in this meadow will lead you on, with a hedge close by on your right. Passing by another three-way sign, also on the right, walk on by the hedge. This will bring you to a wicket gate at a way sign. Go through into the area which contains a seat and St Peter's restored well.

Coming out onto a lane, turn left. A house, St Peter's Well, will then be on the right. Walk on up the lane. A flight of steps will soon be on your left, leading up to the church – a lovely 14th century building. Leave on the path to the lychgate. Going out onto the lane through the lychgate and opposite Church Cottage, turn left. Walk up to the road junction and, with The Old Nursery on the left, bear right onto the road. You will need to take care on this short section as there is no pavement. Passing Lodsworth Polo Shop on the right, you will shortly be back in the centre of the village. If your timing is right, cream teas can be obtained from the stores opposite the pub.

Lurgashall
The Noah's Ark

Lurgashall is one of the very few places in Sussex which can truly be described as being untouched by development – and long may it remain so. The Noah's Ark was built as a pub in 1450 and unlike so many others, its name has never been changed. It must surely be part of one of the most beautiful rural villages in the whole of Sussex, set on the edge of the village green, with its neighbour the 1,200 year old parish church of St Laurence. The pub itself is a delight, the pride and joy of its owner, Kathleen Swannell. The whole of the comfortable interior sparkles with care and attention. Similar care goes into the choice and preparation of the home-cooked food offered. A children's room is available, with walkers being especially welcome.

Telephone: 0428 707346.

How to get there: Lurgashall lies approximately 6 miles north of Petworth and is reached by turning west on an unlisted road off the A283, Petworth to Godalming road. Alternatively, there is a cross country route leaving the A286 road, turning east at Fernhurst. However, please note that both of these roads are very narrow and need to be negotiated with caution.

Parking: The pub's car park is available to customers while they walk. Alternatively there is a lot of adjacent grass verge space which may be used.

Length of the walk: 3 miles. Maps: OS Landranger 197, Pathfinder SU 82/92 (inn GR 937272).

Despite its proximity to the Surrey hills and the nearness of Blackdown (919 ft) – you will go by the foot of it – there are no hills along this route, which is over gently undulating farmland and has some delightful woodland tracks along the way. This area was much beloved by Alfred Tennyson, the poet (1809 – 1892) who lived on the south-facing slope of Blackdown. He and his family used St Laurence's parish church in the village, which bears many memorials to the poet, and indeed the war memorial bears witness to the loss of Aubrey and Harold Tennyson along with many other local men in the 1914/18 War. This place, with its lovely old buildings of Saxon origin has an unusually large number of yew trees within the churchyard, as you will see when you end the walk there.

The Walk
Assuming that you have left your car at the pub, walk west on the lane, with the pub on your right and the green on your left, then the cricket pavilion and Meadowside Cottage, both on the right. Still on the lane, bear to the right and just round the corner, turn right over a stile at a way sign. In a few yards, this narrow path, which is enclosed by wire fences, takes you past a bungalow on the left. After the bungalow, go over a stile (glance back from this point for a good view of the church steeple across the fields). Continue on through a gateway into a field, on the other side of which go over a stile. The way continues on a woodland track through Spring Coppice, so named as the area contains coppiced chestnuts. You will continue for some way on this very pretty woodland track, clearly discernible. Pass by a two-way sign on the right, going over a stile. Some way beyond you will be approaching a fence

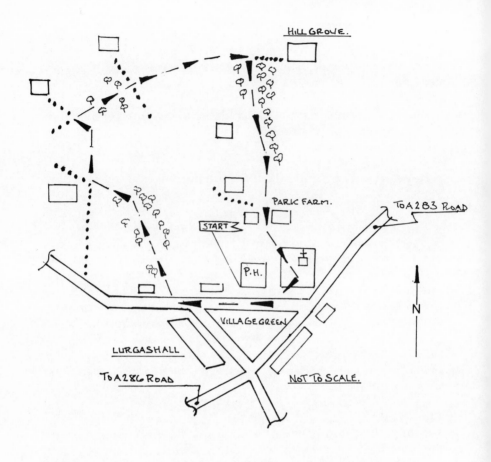

across the track. Go over the stile here, with a two-way sign on the right. On your left at this point you will see another wide track, a two-way sign, buildings and a number of caravans. Now in a field, walk straight on with trees and a hedge on the left.

Coming to the end of the line of trees on the left in this field, the path goes between two trees, across a dry ditch and embankment, into the next field. Go over a railway sleeper bridge and turn left just beyond it, over a stile at a two-way sign. Still with a hedge on the left, walk on to the three-way sign already in view and turn right on reaching it. In taking this northerly direction, you will catch sight of a large hill. This is Blackdown and the Temple of the Winds, so named by

The war memorial at St Laurence's church, Lurgashall.

Tennyson. From where you are now standing, there is a building called Hobstevens in front of you and, looking to the right of it, about halfway up on the face of Blackdown, you will see a large house, Aldsworth, where the poet lived.

The path continues from the way sign across the field, heading for trees. Then, with a two-way sign on the right, going over a stile into a wood, the path descends very steeply to a footbridge and leaves it, climbing steeply and bearing right, heading out of the wood and into a field. Shopp Hill Farm House will be on rising ground across the field to the left. With a hedge on the right, walk across this field and go through a gateway in the hedge in front of you at a four-way sign, (ingoring the gate and stile here on the right). You will now be in a narrow field, with a timber fence on the left and a hedge on the right. Go through an area with some trees, over a footbridge and then a stile into another field – still with the continuing hedge and occasional trees on the right.

At the next gate, go over the stile, there to continue into yet another field. As you progress across it, some of the buildings of Hillgrove hamlet will come into view. Climb the next stile at a gate and this will bring you into a clearing. Walk straight on and go over yet another stile at a gate which takes you on to a woodland path. Here, on your left, will be a series of ponds, much favoured by the local mallard duck population. Passing the last of the ponds, go over a stile, then, almost immediately, with a three-way sign on the left, turn right. Cross a plank bridge into the woodland path through Upper Barn Hanger. Cross a further plank bridge spanning a brook which acts as a drain from the ponds on your left. The path will start to bear to the right, away from the brook. Here you need to be vigilant. The path will suddenly turn to the right, taking you over a stile at a gate and way sign where you then turn left into a field. The path follows the woods, which are close by on the left.

You now simply follow the path skirting the woods on the left. It will take you over three more stiles and across four more fields. Along the way, on the right, you will pass by some buildings, one a converted barn.

Finally, you come to the fourth stile. Go over it to re-enter the wood and here you need to watch for the next way sign, which is only a few yards from the last stile and will be on your right. Do not be confused by a sunken track which goes off to the left. The footpath will very soon drop down steeply to a footbridge, climbing up the opposite bank. If you walk here in autumn, take care as this bridge becomes very slippery with wet leaves. At the top, go over a stile at a two-way sign and turn right. As you mount the last stile, you will see the steeple of St Laurence's church at Lurgashall rising above the fields. Walk on the few yards to the other side of the field and, in the corner at a two-way sign, turn left. (Do not go through the gate there.) Now with a hedge on the right, walk on down the field. Farm buildings will be on the right beyond the hedge. Go over a stile into the next field and, still with the hedge on the right and coming to a gate, go over the stile there and walk out on to the farm track just beyond, to the three-way sign, and turn left.

Soon, the buildings of Park Farm will come into view. Walk on. As you come to a fork, bear right and the farm ponds will be on your left and right. We claim this to be the most picturesque farmhouse setting in West Sussex. Very shortly, turn left, then right – through a gate at a way sign into a field, on the other side of which is the church. Crossing the field, go over a double stile to come out into the churchyard. The exit is to your right and brings you out opposite the pub.

8 Halfway Bridge
The Halfway Bridge Inn

The Halfway Bridge Inn was built in 1710 as a post house, horse-changing and refreshment stop for stage-coaches using this busy east-west artery. The character of the old place has been maintained and the various fireplaces have survived, with the atmosphere enhanced by the period furniture used in the bars. In recent years, one old bricked-up cellar was brought back into use which, we were reliably informed, contains a 'presence'.

Sheila and Edric Hawkins with their sons, Simon and James, own and run this lovely old place in partnership. The food attracts many compliments and is supported by a wide choice of wines. There is a large garden, ideal for family parties on a summer's day, and it is a pleasant place to have a pub meal. Children are welcome in the pub, although children's meals are not provided at reduced prices.

Telephone: 0798 5281.

How to get there: Halfway Bridge lies alongside the A272 road, about midway between Petworth and Midhurst. It is a tiny hamlet now bypassed by the new section of the trunk road, but is accessible by slip roads, part of the old carriage way, from either direction.

Parking: The pub itself has only a fairly small car park. This however, is no problem as there is plenty of space in the old road at the back. The pub's parking space may be used, with permission, by customers while they walk.

Length of the walk: 4¼ miles. Maps: OS Landranger 197, Pathfinder SU 82/92 (inn GR 931220).

The walk goes through Lodsworth churchyard, with its magnificent trees, and then visits the hamlet of River. You will follow the deep gorge of the river Lod on your return to Halfway Bridge.

The Walk
The present-day back of the pub has two houses opposite, one called Bridge Cottage, whilst the other (not named) has its woodwork painted in the yellow favoured by Cowdray Estates. It is between these two dwellings that you start off on this walk and, within a few yards, the track will take you by farm buildings on the right. Continue up this gently climbing track and soon you will see, in front of you, some of the houses of Lodsworth. With a three-way sign on the left, walk on into the right-hand fork of the track.

With Manor Cottage, a red-brick and tiled building, on the left, continue into its approach drive (sunken track) and just beyond, Manor Farm will be on your left, with Lodsworth church directly in front and Manor House on the right. Walk across the grass and go through a wooden gate set in the church boundary wall. Bear left into the churchyard, which will put you on to the paved church path taking you out through the lychgate. Turn right on to the lane which will take you by St Peter's Well House on your left. Just beyond this, bear right on to the little green containing a seat and St Peter's Well. Go through the wicket gate at the way sign.

Keeping the hedge close by on the left, turn right across the meadow at the three-way sign. The broad field path will bring you to Eel Bridge over the river Lod, where, in times

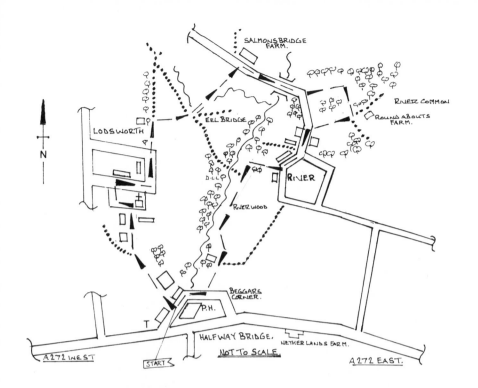

past, traps were set to catch eels and elvers.

At the approach to the bridge and gate with a four-way sign on the right, turn left to go over a stile only a few yards away in the fence. The clear path across this meadow leads to a double stile. Go over it into another meadow, keeping the trees and stream close by on the right. You will walk into a cluster of blackthorn and other trees and, once clear of these, bear left to the next stile at a two-way sign. This path, now passing through woodland, will go over a plank bridge and shortly afterwards, a stile. Keeping the stream and trees on your right, go over the next stile and a plank bridge. Climbing yet another stile, at a way sign, you will come to a large meadow. Walk up the rising ground and, reaching the crest, the building of Salmonsbridge Farm will be to your front. Walk on to the field gate. Go over the stile, turning right on to River Lane. Cross over Salmons Bridge (named after Miss Salmon who, in the 11th century held the licence for the toll bridge). At

Victorian post-box, Lodsworth.

an acute bend in the lane, turn left into the waymarked woodland path.

This meandering path will bring you to a two-way sign. Turn right and the track continues uphill into the woods at the top of the rise. Reaching a three-way sign, bear right and, coming to a junction of four tracks, go under the power lines and straight on. You will then be walking under a single power cable. As you come out on to a farm track, a four-way sign will be in front of you. Turn right just before reaching it. The path continues through the woods. At a two-way sign, on your left, bear right on to a metalled driveway and, passing an ancient oak tree, the drive now comes out on to River Lane. Turn left and walk on down the lane, passing various impressive houses, including Keepers Mead and Rope Makers. A way sign and Victorian wall post-box are all on the right, as are Audley House and Woolgers. Just beyond, turn right at the way sign.

This downhill path turns left at a two-way sign. Coming to a three-way sign on the left, bear left into the continuing woodland track. Ignoring a track going off to the right, go straight on to pass a two-way sign on your left. The track continues now above the deep ravine of the river Lod on your right. You will follow this for some way and eventually the track will start to climb gently and, at the top of this rise, you will come to a large house. The track will continue between it and a three-way sign. Walk on down to the old road (Beggars Corner) and turn right. Going over a bridge (Halfway Bridge) you will see the pub and hamlet in front of you.

Slindon
The Spur

The Spur, which started life as the 'Sir George Thomas', was built during the 1600s although the precise date is unknown. It would have served as a horse-changing and victualling stop for coaches to and from London and the south coast towns. It is a large, comfortable pub, welcoming in all seasons. For those walkers who prefer cooler weather, this house is particularly attractive in winter, with its large double-sided fire, where a selection from the extensive bar menu can be enjoyed. Bar food, which is a speciality here, includes substantial meals ranging from traditional English dishes to those of Continental style. The restaurant is a delight, furnished in keeping with the general air of its past and a comfortable place in which to enjoy a more formal meal. Reservations are recommended if you want to eat in the restaurant on a Sunday. The pub has a large, safe garden. Parents and families are made very welcome, something that the landlord, Clive Smith, and his wife are keen to encourage.

Telephone: 0243 814216/814635.

How to get there: The pub is situated on the A29 Bognor to London road, 1½ miles north of Fontwell race course.

Parking: Outside the pub a section of the old road has been retained, part of which has been divided off into car parking spaces. Alternative parking may be possible by the grass verge.

Length of the walk: 4¾ miles. Maps: OS Landranger 197, Pathfinder SU 80/90 (inn GR 971082).

This walk is over undulating countryside through wood and parkland. The whole area offers an almost unlimited choice for walking, at any season. It is quite deliberately routed through the northern section of Slindon village, which is largely owned by the National Trust, and this short glimpse will, hopefully, lure you back again. Of particular interest (and on the route) is The Old Bakery where, in the season, cream teas are available and opposite to it is the Old Post Office – a step back in time.

The Walk

From the pub, walk north beyond the filling station, and continue on to the footpath sign a short distance ahead. Turn right over the stile, going down a series of steps, and, in fairly quick succession, go over two more stiles to emerge onto a broad track opposite a five-bar gate and three-way sign. Turn right. On your left will be a Scout hut and campsite.

Pass by, on your right, a two-way sign. The track, climbing gently, will come to another three-way sign, again on your right. A few yards beyond and on your right are three concrete (SV) sluice valve markers and in a few steps you will be in a clearing with a junction of three tracks. Bear left into the one with a pole gate across it.

This stony track, climbing gently, will continue on for about ¾ mile through Rewell Wood, coming eventually to a junction of four tracks. At the three-way sign there turn left, down the fairly steep face of Rewell Hill. Having passed a one-way sign on the way down, you will then come to a two-way sign and emerge on to open ground. Turn left. You will be approaching a very clear junction of grass paths – turn left. The A29 (Fairmile Bottom) road is below and parallel to you.

Continue on towards a solitary yew tree on the Downside

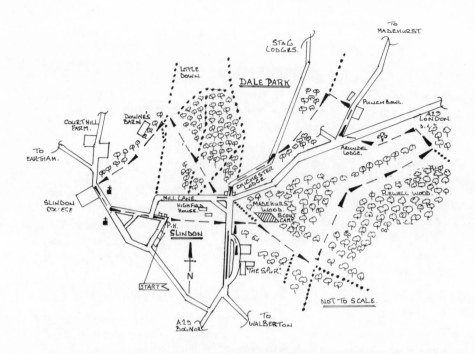

and, just beyond it, turn right on another grass path down to the
road. You will now see the lane junctions of Arundel Lodge and
Madehurst village. Cross, with care, over the road, turning right
into Madehurst Lane. Pass by the entrance drive of Punch Bowl
and just beyond, on the left, turn left between Dale Park
boundary wall and a flint-built house. Go through the timber
gate facing you into Dale Park. Walk up this short section of
field, with a fenced wood on the left, and, at the top, turn left
at a three-way sign into the wood on a farm track. In only a few
yards, and going by a two-way sign, the clear grass track heads
towards another copse. Walk towards it and, with it on your
right, continue around it. Coming to a two-way sign, turn left.

   In only a few yards down this stony track, turn right on to a
clear path across a narrow section of field. The same path will
continue on by another wood on your left. This will come out
on to Dale Park House drive. Turn left at the way sign and walk
on to Chichester Lodge. When you reach it, go through the
gateway and turn right into the lane to Slindon. In about 300
yards, turn right at a way sign into a woodland path and

52

Post office, Slindon.

continue along its length, passing by two four-way signs, both on the right. This path will then emerge on to open ground, with a wood on your right. Reaching the top of the rise of this field, walk on, passing a three-way sign.

Coming now to a four-way sign and also the southern entrance of the Bignor Hill Bridle Road, both on the right, continue straight on with a fence on your right. A short distance further on, a three-way sign will be on your left. Turn left, walk over to it and turn left onto the cart track which is furthest beyond the way sign. No doubt you will have seen the National Trust sign here which requests 'Please keep all dogs on their leads'. This only applies if you are turning right at this sign. In only a short distance down the track, you will come to Downe's Barn and its stockyard. Looking to the right here you should be able to see Nore Hill Folly across the valley. Beyond the barn (and according to the season of the year) you might catch a glimpse, below you on the right, of Court Hill Farm and farmhouse, the latter the home for a short time of Hilaire Belloc. Reaching a gate across the track, with Slindon College opposite, go out on to the road and turn left.

Only a short way beyond the college, and passing by St Richard's RC church, bear left into Top Road. As you do so you will, no doubt, see the tower of St Mary's church on your right, a few steps away down Church Hill. This lovely old building is well worth a visit. By the same token, so is the rest of this National Trust-owned village. Carry on along Top Road. Should you do this walk in the autumn, cottage No 4 will be a blaze of colour, with pumpkins of different species. Still bearing left, Slindon Pottery will be on your right. Going round the bend in Top Road, the Newburgh Arms will be in front of you, first passing The Old Bakery, which serves teas, and, opposite, the post office, from where you can purchase a copy of *Slindon Village History and Guide*, by Josephine Duggan Rees.

Walk on towards the Newburgh Arms and continue into the pathway between it and the houses on your left. This will bring you out into the village recreation area. Continue beyond it on to a field path. In front will be Highfield House and over to your right the Spur. The steps at the end of this path will bring you out on to the grass verge of the A29. On your right the Spur awaits you.

10 Offham
The Black Rabbit

Reputed to be the only Black Rabbit in the country, this inn's precise construction date is unknown. As with so many other old buildings, the original deeds and records have long since 'disappeared', but it can be assumed that it would have been built in the latter half of the 18th century. The choice of its site was not a particularly wise one as it was often subject to flooding and, very occasionally, this is still the case. The first recorded licensee was a John Oliver in 1804. He was a man with an eye for business as he supplied beer and victuals to the navvies and quarrymen employed in digging the various 'cuts' and alterations to the natural course of the river Arun, designed to relieve the flooding in the area between Pulborough and Arundel. The pub's business was supplemented at a later date by nearby railway construction. During both periods the place had a bad reputation for drunkenness and violence, a marked difference to its demeanor today.

Food is available all day in the holiday season, via a self-service cafeteria, with cream teas served in the afternoon. This is a particularly pleasant place to sit by the riverside to have a meal at any time of day. The large, more formal, restaurant is open all year round. A special feature of the Black Rabbit is the play area for children, where they can be left under supervision. Telephone: 0903 882828.

How to get there: The Black Rabbit at Offham is situated about a mile north-east of Arundel town centre and can only be reached by taking the road (Mill Road) to Swanbourne Lake, one of the entrances to Arundel Park, where just beyond is the entrance to the Wildfowl and Wetlands Reserve. This road continues to South Stoke. The sliproad to the pub branches to the right just beyond the wildfowl reserve.

Parking: There is space for a large number of cars just beyond the pub. The current managers, Martin and Jill Earp, with their deputy, Adam Wilson, are happy for walkers to use it, providing the pub is patronised.

Length of the walk: 4½ miles. Maps: OS Landranger 197, Pathfinder TQ 00/10 (inn GR 025085).

The walk through Arundel Park can only be described as spectacular, particularly on the section which first enters the park through the Lion and Unicorn gate at Offham Lodge. The further you walk along the climbing embankment beside the farm track, the wider the views will extend across the Arun valley and to the east. We would be surprised if you could resist the temptation to rest awhile and absorb the beauty of the place . . . You can be sure of one thing, there will not be too many people around.

Reaching the highest point, where you turn off between two plantations of trees and change direction, the views will be to the south, across the park and over the English Channel — and it will be all downhill. At Swanbourne Lake you can, if you wish, stop for refreshment before setting out for the last section of the walk, taking you along by the Wildfowl Trust and out onto the river Arun bank path.

A family walk, indeed, but not for dogs. Please note that dogs are not permitted in Arundel Park.

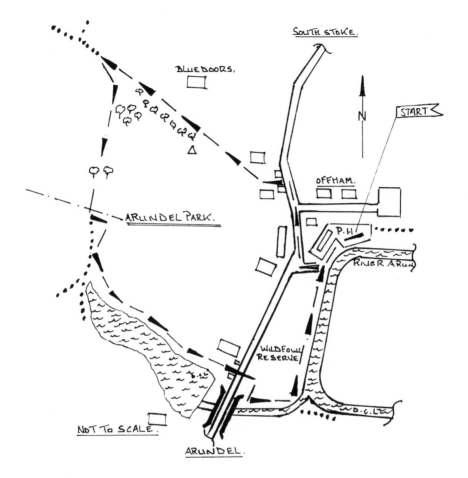

The Walk

From the car park walk back out to the South Stoke road and turn right on to it. Old Quarry Cottages will then be on your left, with the rear of the pub on the right. You would be advised to keep to the right-hand side of the road here and walk in single file to face the oncoming traffic. At the road junction, turn left (still on the South Stoke road) and continue up to Offham Lodge gates. The Lion and Unicorn gate with the lodge house was built in 1850, but sadly, the unicorn is now minus his horn. Cross over the cattle grid into the park. Having passed by the bungalow on your right, and in order to take advantage of the

Mill Road Lodge, entrance to Arundel Castle.

views, leave the rough stone track and walk on top of the embankment which runs parallel to the track below – you will be making for a single tree on the bank, which you will pass on your left. As you continue uphill you will enjoy marvellous views to your right.

You will come to a crossing track – walk straight on over it. The right-hand branch goes down to Blue Doors, an estate house which you will see below you. On your left you may see the Ordnance Survey triangulation point at the high point of these immediate hills (349 ft).

Now approaching 'Dry Lodge Plantation', go through the timber gate set across the track and continue ahead, still with the fenced plantation on your left. Go through a second gate across the track and start bearing off to your left, with the plantation still close by on the left. As you round the end of the enclosed trees there will be a way sign on the left. Now on a broad grassy track, you will soon come to another way sign, again on the left. Here you will turn right off the track on to the Downside, across which there is no perceptible sign of a path. Ahead of you will be a group of trees – continue on by these

58

on your left. A fence will be down on your right. A whole new vista opens up before you, reaching across the park to the coastal plain and the Channel.

You will now be heading towards two isolated trees on the Downside in front of you. When you reach this landmark, walk away from it and continue beyond, keeping the two trees directly behind you and soon in front of you a fence will come into view. Set within this fence you will see a stile at a way sign. Go over the stile and turn directly left, instead of continuing in the direction of the way sign. You will find this way less steep. With the fence now on the left, go down to the track below. Turn right at the gate and walk ahead to a three-way sign and turn left on to a wide grass track.

You will now pass, on the right, a two-way sign and shortly beyond this you will be at the head of Swanbourne Lake. Go over a cattle grid at a gateway and way sign and walk straight ahead on the stony track. Do not turn right into the other path going around the lake. The path you are on will eventually bring you to Swanbourne Lodge, serving food in the holiday season. There are toilets here also. Now go through the wicket gate and cross straight over the road to a small gravel area from which two paths lead. Take the right-hand path. On your left will be the enclosure fence of the Wildfowl and Wetlands Reserve. Coming to the Mill Stream bank path, the foot/road bridge will be on the right. Turn left on to the stream bank path, which will take you out onto the river Arun bank path. Here, again, turn left. The Black Rabbit pub will be in front of you. At the end of this path the way sign will direct you through the children's play area and the end of your walk.

⑪ Burpham
The George and Dragon

This purpose-built pub, constructed in 1730, is largely unchanged since that time. It remained in the ownership of one family, the Wests, up until 1930. At that time, because of the Depression, they were forced to sell to Henry and Constable, the Arundel brewers. The Wests stayed on as tenants and with the death of the last male member, George West, his two sisters (Ada and Gertrude) continued until they both died in 1945. It is claimed that the 'presence' of a deceased West is still in residence – a niece of the two sisters who pre-deceased them and whose portrait as a young girl now hangs in the bar. The pub had connections with the smuggling trade and, as evidence of that, a 'spinning jenny' (a device to establish equal portions of the loot) is still fixed to the ceiling of what is now the restaurant. A door in the same room once led into a tunnel down to the river.

The present owners, George and Marianne Walker, run a well ordered comfortable establishment, where Marianne's

Continental background is immediately apparent in the style, presentation and service of the food. Traditional bar and restaurant menus are also available, and all is of excellent quality. Children's portions are available at adjusted prices. Telephone: 0903 883131.

How to get there: The George and Dragon at Burpham (pronounced 'Burfham') is reached by turning north off the A27 just east of Arundel and north of Arundel railway station at the foot of Mount Lavinia, signposted to 'Warningcamp, Wepham and Burpham'.

Parking: There is none which is specific to the pub. However, the local recreation field immediately behind the George and Dragon has a large 'free' car parking area available to all.

Length of the walk: 3½ miles. Maps: OS Landranger 197, Pathfinder TQ 00/10 and TQ 01/11 (inn GR 039089).

This walk has lovely views and the added bonus of being able to look across the Arun valley at the turrets and keep of Arundel Castle (usually in silhouette). The views expand as you approach Peppering High Barn. A steep downhill footpath takes you to the bank path of the river Arun for your return route to Burpham. Back in the village, you may like to visit the ancient church, St Mary's, mentioned in Domesday, and the site of the fort, built in King Alfred's time to repel marauding parties of Danes coming up from the sea in their long ships.

The Walk
Walk back out to the pub and across the road. With Burpham House on your right, go into the churchyard. At the end of the house wall on your right, turn right and walk over to the churchyard's eastern boundary wall and, going over a stone stile set in it, a way sign will be on your left. Now on a footpath flanked by fences and a hedge, you will pass on the right, a vineyard. This path will eventually emerge onto a lane, where you turn left at the way sign. Climbing gently and passing a farm track on the left which goes down to Peppering Farm, continue on to Peppering High Barn Farm – with magnificent views now on either hand. Pause for a moment to look back to

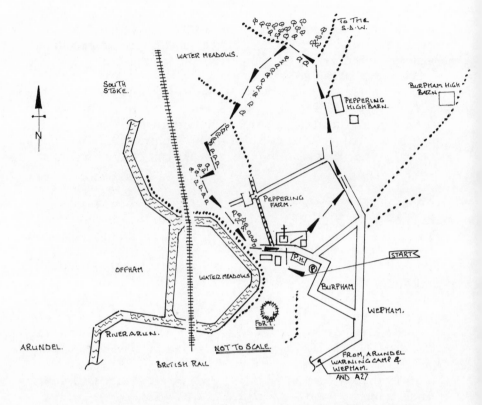

the south-west and the lovely view to Arundel Castle across the Arun valley.

Just beyond the farm buildings, pass by a three-way sign on the left. At another three-way sign on the same side, turn left over the stile and in a few paces go over yet another stile. The footpath goes between wire fences with a hedge on the left. Climb two more stiles in quick succession, beyond which the path drops very steeply for a short way and you should proceed with caution.

Safely descended, go over a stile at a three-way sign and turn left through a metal gate into a delightful wide, grassy farm track. On your left will be trees, whilst on the right an extensive area of watermeadow and wetlands. This supports a large resident population of herons. In the migration season this area is an important feeding ground for many thousands of wildfowl.

Arundel Castle.

Continuing to a three-way sign on your right, walk on to a further three-way sign which will then be in view. Turn right over this and bear left into a meadow. There will then be elder and blackthorn trees on your left. Continue, with these close at hand, around this meadow until you come to another two-way sign which leads you into another meadow. A hedge will be on your left and, on the far side of this meadow, ahead of you, will be a stand of mature oak trees. Beyond these trees is a wire fence and the buildings of Peppering Farm. Turn right at the wire fence and continue along it to a corner where you turn left. Continue for a short way, with a hedge on your right. This path leads to a two-way sign at a stile and gate. The Arun bank path is on your right and in only a few paces, at a three-way sign, walk on beyond a stile at a gate. Cross over the track leading up to Peppering Farm.

Bearing right, go over another stile at a gateway. This will take you into a long, narrow meadow where you will have the choice of either walking its length or using the river bank path on your right. Before long, Burpham church tower will come into sight. Eventually, at the end of the meadow, you will be forced to use an obvious path. It will take you through scrub woods and over a stile to a fork of paths. Turn into the left-hand one which will bring you to the village blacksmith's shop, once owned by George West of the George and Dragon who was also the village farrier. Shortly beyond this you will be back at the pub.

Houghton
The Bridge Inn

The Bridge Inn enjoys one very important distinction on the subject of access, it lies directly below the main line (Bognor-London/Victoria) railway station at Amberley and is still used extensively by rambling clubs from Surrey and London to reach the many miles of tracks and footpaths available in this area.

The pub started life as a farmhouse, it is thought, around 1740, and it is likely that it changed its role to an alehouse in the late 1700s or early 1800s, for the same economic advantages as its downriver neighbour the Black Rabbit at Offham. For here it sat on another gold mine – an inexhaustible supply of chalk, which could be widely and easily transported by rail and barge, for railway, canal construction and river course alteration. The chalk quarry operators 'Pepper and Sons' were the major suppliers of lime in West Sussex to the building trade. All that commercial hustle and bustle has long gone and this tiny place is now a considerable tourist attraction with the old quarries now being home to the Amberley Chalk Pits Museum. This houses a wide range of exhibits, from railway locomotives to pottery and brick-making, and the museum also has a tea and coffee shop.

The former clientèle of the Bridge Inn, whilst no doubt being easily able to recognise their beer house, could not possibly have imagined the extent and variety of its drink and food. The modern day owner, Stephen Chandler, is justifiably proud of the quality of the food served in his pub, which is based on fresh produce cooked the same day to order, on the premises. Seafood dishes are a speciality. The pub has a large walled garden where children under 14 can be fed and entertained. Opposite the pub is the Boathouse Bar and Restaurant, whilst across the road is the Riverside Tea Garden.

Telephone: 0798 831619.

How to get there: Houghton lies approximately 5 miles northeast of Arundel and about 6 miles west of Storrington, from where it can be reached by using the B2139 road which branches off the main A283. From the west the same B2139 turns east off the A29, Bognor to London Road, at Whiteways Lodge, at the junction with the A284 from Arundel.

Parking: The landlord is quite happy for his space to be used by walkers who will use his facilities. There is also a big parking area available up at the railway station which is subject to a charge during weekdays (free at weekends).

Length of the walk: 3¾ miles. Maps: OS Landranger 197, Pathfinder TQ 00/10 and TQ 01/11 (inn GR 026118).

A fascinating walk, with 80% of the distance on the banks of the river Arun, the route being, as a consequence, almost flat. The riverside paths can be muddy after rain – no problem if you are well shod.

You will also go through the farming communities of North and South Stoke, with their interesting churches. Many very important archaeological finds have come to light in the area, notably at North Stoke where an ancient British dug-out canoe, hewn from an oak tree and 34 ft long, was discovered and can now be seen in the British Museum. If your interests extend to ornithology then you will not be disappointed. The whole area, which is complementary to the Amberley Wild Brooks, is an important wetland staging and feeding site, vital to many wildfowl (sometimes very rare and exotic species) on their world travels. The final stretch is through the riverside trees of South Wood and passing an old disused chalk quarry where one of the old lime-burning kilns still survives.

The Walk

If you have parked at the pub, then walk back out to the B2139 road junction. If you have chosen to park at the railway station, then simply walk down to the road junction. Despite the fact that you will be able to see your first way sign on the bridge from where you are, I would advise crossing over the road to face the oncoming traffic.

On reaching the way sign, turn left and cross the stile at the gate there. Go over the footbridge spanning the 'cut' to turn right over a stile at a gate on to the first section of the river bank path. After some way, go over a stile to turn left at a two-way sign only a few yards away into a narrow enclosed path. As you turn here you will see the buildings of North Stoke across the fields. This path wanders on and eventually comes to a gate where, as you approach it, you will see a house in front of you. Go through this gate. There is a way sign here – turn right onto the lane (Stoke Road). The house, Sloe Cottage, is now on your left. The first buildings you approach, as you continue up the lane, will be a group of estate houses.

A short way further on, and coming to a T-junction, you have a decision to make. The lane leading to the right is signposted to North Stoke church (an old building which is well worth a visit). Despite the fact that the church is now redundant, Mr and Mrs Lake, at North Stoke Farm House next to the church, will be happy for you to borrow the key.

Assuming that you decided to make the short detour to the church, return to the lane junction and, with the flint cottages and the telephone box on your right, walk on beyond them to turn right, going over a stile at a way sign. The flint cottages and their gardens are on your right.

As you walk down this field path, the northern slopes of Arundel Park, and Houghton Hill to the right of it, come into full view. It was down the track over the latter, now the B2139 road, that Charles Stuart rode in 1651 with his companions after his defeat at the Battle of Worcester. The party stopped for food

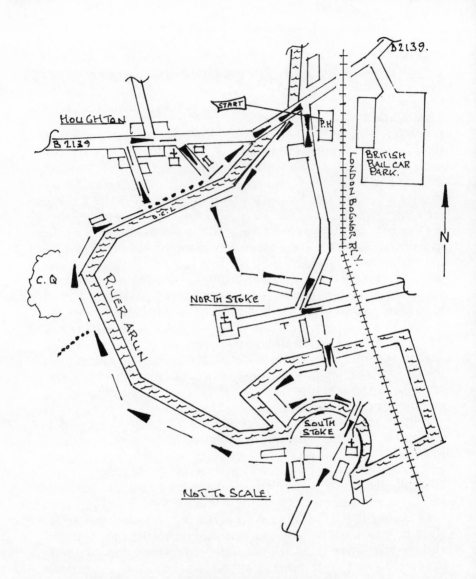

and rest at the George and Dragon at Houghton and probably a change of horses – no doubt commandeered – and would have been paid for by Royalist sympathisers in the area. This journey through Sussex would have been made on the sheep runs and drove roads now known as The South Downs Way to

Brighton (Brighthelmstone) where the party embarked for France and exile.

Go over two more stiles, either side of a farm track. The buildings of North Stoke Farm are on your right. Walk down this field. You will also catch a glimpse of the spire of South Stoke church. Coming to a metal gate, go over the stile there and walk on to the footbridge only a short distance ahead. Cross over this elaborate structure. You will now be on a raised path which will wander on through woods and have wide ditches on either hand. After some way, the buildings of South Stoke Farm will appear on the right through the trees and, shortly after, bear left over a stile on to the 'Arun Bank Path' at a two-way sign. The hamlet and church at South Stoke are now in full view across the river. Walk on to the bridge, turning right over the stile at the three-way sign. Passing another three-way sign on the right at the other end of the bridge, you come onto the lane passing through the hamlet. First, you will reach the entrance to St Leonard's church. This lovely old building is still in use – candle power and all! You will (hopefully) find a small pamphlet for sale covering the history of both church and hamlet. Then, with cottages on the left (No 38 was the pub), walk on. The buildings of South Stoke Farm will be on your right, including the handsome red-brick, five-arched Chapel Barn. Walk on past the farm entrance drive and, just beyond, turn right into the signposted bridleway. Soon you will be alongside Chapel Barn, on the right and just beyond it, turn left at the way sign on the same side, into a wide farm track. On the right will be a modern asbestos-built barn, beyond which the track goes through a muddy farmyard. You will then be on a wide grassy track, with a hedge on the right. You will see the river both beyond and below you.

The track will descend to a gate at a two-way sign. Go over the stile, taking you right into a field. Keep the trees and fence on your right and walk on up the rising ground. With a timber fence on your right, and lovely views across the Arun river valley, you will come to another gate at a two-way sign. Go over the stile here. The track beyond will descend down to river level. Along this path from here, you will need to watch out for tree roots across the path. Now in South Wood, the boundary wall of Arundel Park will start to appear on the left. Passing a three-way sign on the left, the river will be close by on your right. Continue straight on, crossing over a fenced culvert. Then, with a notice on the left concerning a rifle range (no longer in use), you will shortly be in the area of the old disused chalk quarry. Just as you enter the area, the surviving brick limekiln will be on your left. The path continues beyond the old quarry, then, passing a flight of steps on the left and way sign on the right, walk on to pass, on the left, a timber bungalow, beyond which is a metal gate. Depending upon the prevailing weather conditions you will now have a choice.

Over to your right you will see a two-way sign on the river bank. If the weather has been dry you will have no problem walking across to it, and bearing left on to the bank path, which you will follow for a short way, to cross a plank bridge into a field. Walk on to a stile and way sign which you will see in front of you on the other side of the field.

If, however, you find, as I did one Christmas Eve after two weeks of continuous rain, the short distance to the way sign impassable, then you have an easy alternative. Carry on through the metal gate – there is a way sign here also and this will bring you into South Lane. Continue to its junction with the B2139 road and here you turn right. I do advise at this point that you cross over this busy road in order to see around the bend ahead. Walk on beyond the road junction signposted to Bury. At the right moment, cross back over the road to face the oncoming traffic. The farmhouse and buildings of Houghton Farm will be on your right. At the entrance to the farm, also on your right, walk into the track going between the parish church on the right and a house on the left. This will take you to a gate (please note, this is not a public right of way, but one which the landowner allows walkers to use). You go through the gate, taking care to secure it behind you. Walk down the field to the river bank and, just beyond the timber (summer) bungalow on your left, turn left over the stile. This, of course, is the same stile you would meet coming along the river bank path.

Follow the direction of the way sign to Houghton Bridge, in clear view in front of you. Go over the stile there to turn right to cross back over the bridge to rejoin your car – or to catch the train – after what, I'm sure, will have been a thoroughly enjoyable walk.

⑬ Bury
The Black Dog and Duck

This still quite rural village, which was the onetime home of John Galsworthy, nestles at the bottom of the Downs. Its pub has a fascinating history. It is a quaint old hotchpotch, half-thatched building which came into being as a dwelling in about 1423. In 1805 (Trafalgar year) it became Ye Olde Special Cider Shoppe and was licensed to sell ale in 1815. John Griffin, the landlord, who knows the Black Dog and Duck's history by heart will, hopefully, one day produce a historical guide to it.

The pub is comfortable and friendly and walkers are especially welcome – to prove it a sign is displayed to encourage them. Children are catered for with reduced food portions and corresponding prices. If you are looking for country cooking this is the place for you, with (surprise, surprise) the speciality of roast duck available in the restaurant.

Telephone: 0798 831485.

How to get there: The Black Dog and Duck is situated at the bottom of Bury Hill off the A29 (Bognor to London) road and is reached by turning off the main road at one of two lanes going into the village, one of which has the White Horse pub on the corner.

Parking: Providing that permission is sought and the pub is patronised, there is no problem in using the pub's car park while you walk.

Length of the walk: 5¼ miles. Maps: OS Landranger 197, Pathfinder TQ 01/11 and SU 81/91 (inn GR 012135).

The walk, in the shadow of the Downs, is over farmland and through two areas of woodland. It has the added attraction of, at one stage, being within a few yards of the Roman villa at Bignor (open March to October).

The Walk

From the pub's car park, walk out onto the lane. A two-way sign will be on your right at the entrance. Cross over to the gravel area of the two cottages opposite, Kesters Cottage and Kesters House. Bearing right by Street Cottage, walk on down this driveway, which will continue between dwellings, Bartons being on the right. Just beyond, walk into a grassy descending path. Coming to a wicket gate at a two-way sign, cross over the A29 (there are good views in either direction to observe oncoming traffic). There is a flint-built house opposite. Go up the embankment, turning left in the service road (the area to the north and west of the house is occupied by glasshouses). In a few yards, turn right at a two-way sign into a farm track.

At the first bend, go over the stile at a metal gate and way sign. Walk up the field, going over the stile facing you, into a rough and rooty path enclosed by fences. The path, descending, goes through woods. Go over the next stile, then the one opposite and a footbridge with a way sign. Bear right across the field to a gate and two-way sign, going over the stile into a field. With a hedge now on your right, continue along its length, turning right over a double stile at a two-way sign. Now in another field, and keeping the hedge close by on your left, walk on, ignoring a stile on your left, to turn left through a metal gate at a way

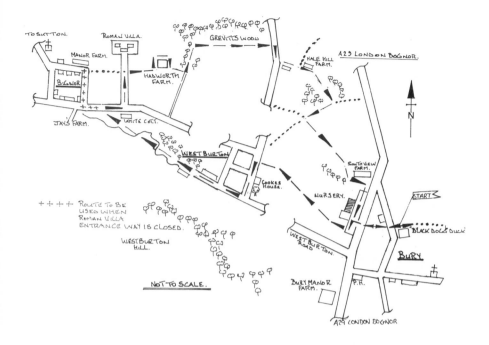

sign. This track, passing a two-way sign on the right, will bring you out onto a lane at West Burton. A large barn will be on your left. Turn left. Farm House Cottages will be on your right.

Walk on down the lane, passing on the left Cookes House, with its huge Lebanese cedar. Passing by a lane junction on the right, walk on and turn right at the next junction. Then, coming to buildings at another junction, walk straight ahead into the lane marked as a cul-de-sac. Just beyond Flints Orchard on the right, walk on to a three-way sign and continue into the path, with Fogdens and a stream on your left. Go over the footbridge, the stream then on your right. This uneven path goes by a notice fixed to a tree, denoting the location of Pill Pond. The footpath goes through a hedge at a two-way sign. Turn right into a field and, with a hedge and stream on the right, follow this round, going over a footbridge at a two-way sign, now in a large field, turning almost immediately left, going over a plank bridge across a drainage ditch. Now with a hedge and stream on your left, continue on the field path. The buildings containing the Roman villa will appear now over to the right. This path

Mosaic at Bignor Roman Villa.

will then make a junction with a wide track across the field. Follow its course, passing a two-way sign on the right. This will bring you out through a gateway onto the Bignor road. Turn right. In only a few yards and opposite a white cottage, turn left into the driveway up to the Roman villa. The mosaic floors, discovered and excavated in 1811, are some of the finest in Britain, and are displayed under cover. There is a museum displaying the Roman artefacts which came to light during excavation. A cafeteria supplies tea, coffee and light meals.

The Roman villa is open every day from 10 am to 6 pm in the summer months (June to September). For opening times, in March, April, May and October telephone 079 87 259. During the open season the entrance driveway may be used by walkers in order to reach the crossing footpath, but it is not itself a public right of way. When it is closed the alternative route up to and through Manor Farm must be used and is indicated by symbols on the sketch map.

At the junction of the villa driveway and the public footpath, with a two-way sign on the left, turn right into the field path leading to Hadworth Farm and, at the farm, follow the direction of three way signs around the buildings to bring you out onto the farm's driveway. At the fourth way sign turn left. At the bend in the drive turn left at a two-way sign into a grassy path and, coming to the end, turn right at a two-way sign into a woodland track. After some way this track will come out on to a lane at a two-way sign. Turn right and walk on the short way to the next way sign on the left, turning left into the track leading to Kymber House and Cottage. At Hale Hill Farm on the left, continue straight on past a three-way sign. Coming next to other buildings on the right, the path continues, still straight ahead, and will bring you to a plank bridge at a two-way sign. Turn right into a woodland path. You will see the previous buildings again through the trees on the right. At the next two-way sign, turn left to leave the woods, going over a stile. Now in a field, turn right. The woods will now be on your right.

In only a few yards turn right through a gateway at a stile in the hedge and fence. The path, now in another field, still follows the woods on your right. Coming then to a three-way sign, turn left over the stile and follow a short section of fence on the left down this field. Where the fence goes off to the left, walk on to a timber power pole and, with this on your left, walk across the continuing field to the hedge in front of you. At the two-way sign here go over a plank bridge into a field. Go over another stile and you will see, in front of you across the field, a two-way sign and gateway, with the buildings of South View Farm beyond. Walk on to the buildings. With these on the left, walk ahead. The silage pits will then be only a few yards to your left and you will be heading for a hedge in front of you, concealed in which is a plank bridge. Go over it, turning left at the two-way sign. Keep close to the hedge on the left, with the farm buildings on your left. The field path will then bring you to a section of concrete roadway going into the farm on your left. Bearing slightly to the right here, walk across the field, going through the gateway at a two-way sign. Shortly beyond, go over a stile at a metal gate at another way sign and turn right into the service road at Bury.

With Arun House, a black and white painted building on your right, walk on up the service road and, coming to the flint house at the top, turn left, going down the embankment and crossing the A29 into the footpath, to retrace your footsteps back into Bury village.

⑭ Kirdford
The Half Moon

Many of the pubs in this series have something in common: that they did not start life with that purpose in mind, and the Half Moon is no exception. Kirdford, in times past, was very rural and, to a certain extent, this is still the case. Because of its inaccessibility, it was, of necessity, self-contained. The collection of buildings which comprise the pub (built in 1640) serviced the local farming community and contained workshops housing blacksmith and farrier, wheel and cartwrights, carpenter's shop and, with the church opposite, the coffin maker. The local farms would have made their own beer and cider, which was available to the farm hands. The lovely old interior of the present day pub still retains the huge fireplace which was used for smoking bacon and hams . . . a delightful hostelry in every respect.

This is a family run pub where the preparation and serving of food is taken very seriously indeed. Despite its inland location, the Half Moon specialises in fresh fish and shellfish and claims

that its various salmon dishes are a must! Both bar and restaurant menus are reasonably priced and extensive. Walkers and their families are made very welcome by the proprietors, Mrs Ann Moran and her son, and the large garden is equipped with a children's play area.
Telephone: 0403 77223.

How to get there: Kirdford lies 5 miles north-east of Petworth town and is reached by taking the unlisted road via Gunters Bridge and Balls Cross at the junction of the A283 and A272 roads.

Parking: There is parking along the front of the pub. Walkers should, however, seek the permission of the proprietors and, providing the pub is patronised, there will be no problem. On road parking is in order but most definitely not in the service road for the houses opposite.

Length of the walk: 4 miles. Maps: OS Landranger 197, Pathfinder TQ 02/21 and SU 82/92 (inn GR 017265).

The walk is very rural, going over farmland and almost totally on flat terrain. An easy stroll, the only challenge being some rutted farm tracks.

The Walk
From the pub walk south down the road (the church will be on your left). Go over the old bridge across the river Kird. On the other side, on the right, is a raised causeway for use when the river floods here. You will pass by Bridge Foot Cottage on the right, then two more cottages. Just beyond the last one, Field Cottage, turn right over a stile at a way sign between the cottage and Kirdford Quail Farm. This will take you around the farm between fences.

Go through a gate set in a paddock fence. Follow the fence, now on your left, across the field. Walk to a hedge in front, behind which is a building. Go through a gate in the hedge at a two-way sign and you will be in another meadow, with Gownfold Farm close by. Keep the farm on your left and walk across the field. Go through a gate in the opposite hedge, turning right at the two-way sign on to a farm track. Continue

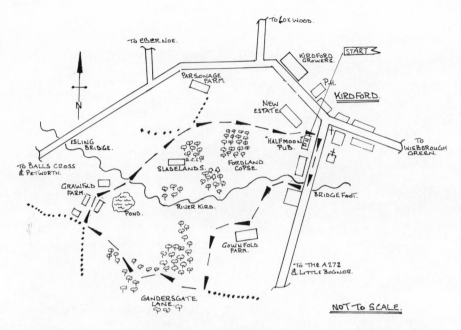

on this track, passing a succession of gates and finally going through a metal gate in front of you. Turn left at the two-way sign and you will be in a very long field. Walk down its length, with the hedge on your left, towards main grid power lines. At a gate set in a hedge, turn right on to a farm track – Gandersgate Lane.

At a three-way junction of tracks, turn right at the three-way sign, shortly beyond which is a similar junction of tracks, but, with a two-way sign in front of you, turn right. After some distance you will see the buildings of Crawfold Farm on your right. With an estate house coming into view, walk on towards it. Reaching a four-way sign, turn right. The house will now be on your left. Walk on down the approach lane to the farm and continue through the buildings. Coming to a fuel storage tank set up on blocks on your right, turn right into the barnyard. The farmhouse will be on your left. Continue beyond the straw barn on your right and, with a large pond in front, bear left around a cart shed on your left. Go through a gateway at a two-way sign. A fence goes partway down this field. Follow it on your right. Walk on to a bridge between two stiles at a two-way sign.

78

Kirdford village signpost.

Go over the bridge into another field. Walk up the rising ground to follow, on your left, the fence – then trees and a hedge. A large house, Sladelands, will appear on your right.

79

At the top of this field, with a pond behind the trees on your left, go through a gateway and almost immediately go over a stile at a two-way sign into a field. Walk down this field to follow the hedge on your left. Coming to a two-way sign at a gate, turn sharp right (this brings the gate and sign behind you). Walk across the field, which will bring you approximately to the middle of the opposite fences, which enclose the track leading from Parsonage Farm to Sladelands. Go over the two stiles at the way signs and continue into the next field. You will be heading towards a hedge. Go through the hedge and gateway at a two-way sign into yet another field. You are approaching the trees of Fordland Copse and a hedge will be on your left.

At a three-way sign on the left, bear right. The path then goes into the wood and will emerge from it at a two-way sign into a field, with the hedge now on the right. Go over the next stile at a two-way sign. The path goes into a field and, with a fence on your right, continue on to go through a gap in the next hedge. Follow the next field path, now with the hedge on your right.

The church and some buildings of Kirdford will appear in front and the buildings of an estate will be on your left across this field. Walk on to a two-way sign, turning left across the field and making for the gateway set in the boundary fence. Once into the estate the path, bearing right, goes through the houses and in a few yards, at a two-way sign, you walk into the rear garden of the Half Moon pub.

Loxwood
The Onslow Arms

The pub, built in 1860, was constructed specifically to serve the barge traffic on the Wey and Arun Canal, which connected London and Chichester, and onwards by sailing barge to Portsmouth. This system was built in 1816, and was therefore a very much later addition to its counterparts in London and the north. The Onslow Arms not only supplied food and drink to the bargees, but was also a horse-changing station. The stable buildings are still there, and what is now the large riverside garden was the area used for changing the horses over – what a busy place it must have been! The pub was built by the Onslow family who resided in the area, one of three of the same name in the surrounding district. One of the survivors of the family still lives in Loxwood. The pub's commercial life, however, was short-lived. By 1868 the canal company had gone into bankruptcy (yes, it happened even in those days). The system rapidly fell into disuse, being officially abandoned in 1871. But there is hope for the revival of the canal yet, with the ambitious, dedicated work already undertaken by the Wey and Arun Canal Trust Limited, established in 1970, which goes from strength to strength with its restoration work.

The licensee, Harry Saint, with his wife Sally, runs a comfortable and friendly pub, where walkers and families are especially welcome. Harry is the chef and justifiably proud of the range and quality of his food, all produced from fresh ingredients. His speciality is steak and kidney pie – wonderful stuff – but with one of the ingredients being King & Barnes high gravity beer, remember the drink/driving laws.

Telephone: 0403 752452.

How to get there: Loxwood lies on the B2133 to the far north of the county close to the Surrey border. It is easily accessible from the A29 at Adversane (south), the A272 at Billingshurst (east), and the A2381 at Alfold Crossways (north).

Parking: There is no problem here with parking while you walk but, naturally, the landlord expects that his permission is sought and his pub patronised.

Length of the walk: 4¼ miles. Maps: OS Landranger 186 and 187, Pathfinder TQ 03/13 (inn GR 042312).

This is a thoroughly lovely walk, which leaves the Onslow Arms by the northbound Wey South Path, itself of considerable interest. (To assist you in this, a leaflet issued by the Canal Trust is available at the pub.) It then changes direction at the junction with the Sussex Border Path and at Oakhurst Farm emerges into beautiful rural Sussex Weald country. It continues down to Brewhurst Mill which, with the hamlet, is one of the prettiest and most interesting of places, and from where it is only ½ mile back to the pub.

The Walk
From the pub car park go back out to the road and turn right, keeping to the pavement on that side. At the first way sign on your right, turn left across the road and walk into the wide entrance of the canal towpath, the Wey South Path. Riverside Cottage will be on your left. In a short distance you will go through a gateway and the towpath continues between the canal and river.

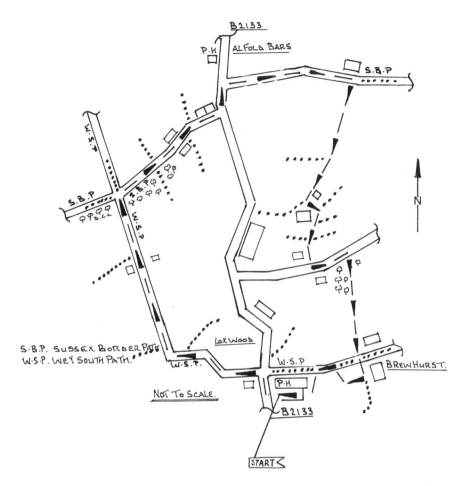

After some way you will reach Devil's Hole lock, bridge and
three-way sign, all of which are on the right. What a sad sight
the ruined lock currently is but, of course, it is on the Canal
Trust's restoration programme. Continue straight on, still on the
towpath, passing on the left another three-way sign. The towpath now becomes quite narrow. Next to appear on your left,
just beyond the river, are some stable buildings, beyond which
the path becomes obstructed with large tree roots running
across it, whilst, again on the left, another stable establishment
will appear. Then a large red-brick period house with a
Horsham stone slab roof will be directly in front of you. As you

draw level with the building you will then go out onto a driveway, the right-hand section of which leads up to another house. Go straight across the driveway, with a three-way sign on your left. Continue, still on the narrow towpath, and go through a wicket gate. The river will no longer be on the left but the towpath will faithfully follow the canal on your right.

With a metal gate now on the right, go through the gate directly in front of you and suddenly you will again have the river for company on the left. Go through a second metal gate and, a short way beyond, turn right at a four-way sign into the eastbound Sussex Border Path, a wide track going through woods for a short way. Coming to another four-way sign, continue through a gate into a field, with the Sussex Border Path heading directly towards Oakhurst Farm. Keep the hedge close by on your left and, upon coming to a gate at a two-way sign, go through it into the farmyard. Needless to say, if you have a dog with you, it must be leashed. This is what we call a *real* farm. The construction of the farmhouse is of particular interest, especially its chimneys. Continue on through the yard, passing, on the right, the duck pond and a three-way sign. Continue into the metalled lane leading away from the farm, still on the Sussex Border Path, and very soon you will be approaching buildings – the village of Alfold Bars. Coming out onto the B2133 road, turn left on to it and walk on the right-hand side of the road as quickly as possible.

In only a few yards, and with the Sir Roger Tichebourne pub on the left, turn right into Pigbush Lane – the continuing Sussex Border Path. Passing the much restored and elaborated Sheaves Farm House on the left, walk on down the lane. Your next landmark, the buildings of Songhurst Farm, will come into view ahead. With this imposing place (no longer a farm) on your left, turn right at the four-way sign, off the Sussex Border Path, into a wide metalled farm track. Quite suddenly you have come out into lovely rolling Sussex Weald farmland with wonderful views to the west and south of the Downs, amongst which, and quite unmistakably, is the huge bulk of Blackdown (elevation 919 ft) which, as its name suggests and when seen from a distance, takes on the colour of its name.

As you continue further down the track, the buildings of Old Songhurst Farm will be on your left across the fields. After some

Pancake Cottage, Loxwood.

way, the single metalled farm track will divide into twin
concrete strips, there passing a three-way sign on the right.
Walk on towards the buildings coming into view ahead,
Songhurst New Farm first with Songhurst Cottage on the left.
Walk just beyond it and, bearing left, turn right over a stile at
a four-way sign, into a field and walk on towards the farm to
continue around the field, with the farm buildings and its timber
fence on your right. Having reached the back of the white
painted farmhouse, carry on down the field path. There will be
a hedge on your right. At the end of this field, go over a stile at
a gateway and, with a three-way sign on the right, walk on, still
on a field path with a continuing hedge on the right. At the next
gate you once again have the choice of using the stile, to go into
the third field. Coming to a four-way sign, the path goes across
this field and you will pass by on your right, two large oak trees.
Also on your right, across the field, will be the northern
outskirts of Loxwood village. Going then through another gate,
you will have a hedge on your right again, with a building in
front. As you continue on by the hedge, a house will then
appear on the other side of it, known as Pancake Cottage. Go

over the stile at a way sign bringing you on to a road. Before turning left, take the opportunity to walk the few yards to the front of Pancake Cottage – as beautiful a building as its name implies, set in lovely gardens full of mature examples of the art of topiary.

Walk east along the lane, passing Little Pancake on the right and the village boundary sign on the same side. Cross over a stream bridge to turn right at a way sign just beyond and go through a gate across the wide track. This wooded area is a great place to see wild daffodils in the spring. In only a short distance down this track you will cross over the canal (Wey South Path). At the four-way sign here you can turn right on to the towpath which will soon take you back to the Onslow Arms. There is, however, a treat in store for you in the form of Brewhurst hamlet and watermill – you can see the buildings from the last way sign.

Walk on towards them and I'm sure you will agree that I do not exaggerate about this being a treat – what a lovely place. As you bear round to the right on the lane, Brewhurst Farm will be on your left, with the restored watermill opposite. You will obviously take your own time here but when you are ready, turn right at the three-way sign by the corner of the mill. Continue the short distance beyond the back of the mill and the path goes over a sluice bridge into a field. Keeping a stream and line of trees close by on the right, walk on around this field, coming then to a stile. Go over it and turn left on to the canal towpath (Wey South Path) at the three-way sign, from where you will shortly be back at the Onslow Arms.

⑯ Nutbourne
The Rising Sun

The building which houses the present day pub was formerly a farmhouse built, it is believed, in the 15th century. It originally stood on one side of the village green, of which, sadly, no trace remains. A licence to sell ale was granted in 1812. Largely unspoilt, the pub has the unusual distinction of retaining its wooden floor in the main bar, giving it a pronounced rural atmosphere, complemented by scrubbed wooden tables.

Janice and Regan Howard welcome children with parents in the pleasant restaurant and in the garden, which is ideal for family groups on warmer days. A comprehensive selection of hot and cold meals is always available, the bar menu concentrating on good, plain food, such as soup and sandwiches. Telephone: 079 88 2191.

How to get there: Nutbourne lies about 2 miles east of Pulborough and can be reached by taking the unlisted road off the A283, signposted 'West Chiltington and Nutbourne'.

Parking: The Rising Sun has no facilities for parking and, like their other customers, walkers will have to use, with discretion, the village street above and below the pub.

Length of the walk: 4 miles. Maps: OS Landranger 197, Pathfinder TQ 01/11 (inn GR 074187).

The walk is quite remarkable in that it goes through the buildings of an old watermill, passes by a disused windmill and, at about the halfway point, crosses what was one of the largest self-contained farms in Sussex, with all the facilities to maintain itself and other neighbouring farms. It is now a private residence. Much of the surrounding land, as you will see, has been converted to vineyards. It is all easy walking.

The Walk
It is easier, regardless of where you are parked, to direct you from the pub. Therefore, facing south, with the pub on your right, walk on down the village street (Nutbourne Street). With Holly Tree Cottage on your right, turn almost immediately left at the way sign. New House will then be on your right. This short section of footpath will lead to a stile at a two-way sign. Turn right over the stile into a fruit farm. Walk on to the next two-way sign and turn left on to a path which goes across a field of soft fruit bushes until you come to a stile in a hedge. Go over the stile and you will see a pond in front of you. At a two-way sign, turn left and the pond will now be on your right.

The path leads directly to the buildings of the watermill, with way signs directing you through and out on to a farm track, where you turn right. Here there is a three-way sign, which is not clearly visible until after you have turned on to the track. The track then continues on with the Nutbourne Vineyards on both sides of it, whilst on your left is a tower which is the remains of the windmill, now converted to a private residence. You will then come to a two-way sign. Go through the gate into a field and there will be a row of poplar trees on your left-hand side. You will come to a stile which takes you over a fence into another field, with a line of cut down poplar trees continuing on the left. You will then go over three more stiles and pass by a two-way sign, before coming out into a drive between two houses.

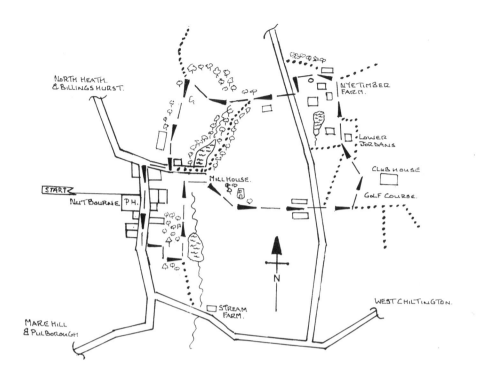

Cross over the lane, which is Gay Street, and climb up the steps cut in the steep bank, before going over the stile at the top into a field, passing a three-way sign on your left-hand side. The path then follows a line of trees on your right-hand side, beyond which there are the buildings of Dennis Marcus Farm. At the end of this field a sign will tell you that you are now on the 'West Chiltington Golf Course'. As you walk along a broad track you will see ahead of you a three-way sign. On reaching it, turn left onto a broad, grassy track and you will then reach a gate. Turn left at the three-way sign on to another grassy track, with a hedge on your right-hand side, crossing over two other tracks. At the end of the field go through a wicket gate into an enclosed footpath leading to a gate. Go through the gate and shortly you will have Lower Jordans on your right, with another house on your left. Leaving the three-way sign on your left, turn right on to a metalled lane, going through a gateway on which is the sign 'Nyetimber'.

The mill stream, Nutbourne

Continue along the lane, leaving a modern house on your left-hand side, until you reach a junction and a three-way sign on your right-hand side. Continue straight on, leaving the boundary wall of Nyetimber Farm on your left-hand side, and you will reach the barns and cart sheds of the farm. At the end of these buildings there is a junction. Turn left onto a farm track and the farm buildings will still be on your left-hand side, with a modern house on your right. As you leave the farm buildings, note the walled storage pit, which is believed to be the only example left in Sussex. The farm track rises for a short distance between large vineyard areas and, when it begins to curve off to the right, you bear off to the left on to a grass path. On your right there is a timber fence, with the vineyard continuing on your left. On reaching a bend in the path, you will be forced to turn to the left and now there will be a hedge on your right-hand side. After about 100 metres, on the right there is a gap in the hedge. Go through the gap and down the steps to a way sign at the bottom. This is Gay Street again and you will be opposite Random Cottage. The footpath continues up the gravel drive between the cottage and its large garages, before crossing the garden to the boundary fence, where there is a wicket gate. Once through the gate, the path is enclosed by a fence and a hedge and you continue along it until you reach a three-way sign on your right. Here you have a choice.

If the path on your right is overgrown, continue along the path until you reach the buildings of Nutbourne watermill and a large pond on your right-hand side. Turn right on to the lane and continue until it reaches Nutbourne Street and you are back at the Rising Sun. This path is indicated by the dots on the sketch map.

If, however, the path on your right is clear, turn right at the way sign and continue along the track through the woods, which does wander about a bit but is fairly easy to follow, until you reach a substantial wooden bridge. After the bridge the path passes several gates and, at one point, you will see a house on the left. A large pond will now be below you on the right and you will soon reach a clearing which has been used to store things like dismantled hen houses and logs. Shortly beyond this area, the path is crossed by another. Turn left at this junction and go over a gate, which has stile steps on either side of it, into a field. The path continues along by a hedge on your right-hand side until it reaches a two-way sign where you go through a gate into another field. The path crosses this field to a stile and two-way sign and then continues into a third field. On your right there is a hedge and then a wall with buildings beyond. You will reach a metal gate which you go through. Facing you is a wall and a two-way sign. Bear left into a tree-lined sunken path and at the end of this you turn right. With Old School House on your left, turn left into Nutbourne Street and you are back at the Rising Sun.

Hammerpot
The Woodman Arms

One of the few pubs left with a thatched roof, which adds to its considerable charm. It was built in 1545 – the year in which the *Mary Rose* sank – starting life as a pair of estate cottages. Then, in about 1740, it was granted an ale licence to become a pub. It was not until 1962 that a full wines, beers and spirits licence was applied for. The interior is authentically old and once inside, you need to take heed of the notice to 'duck not grouse' and save yourself a headache!

Douglas Gilham, the landlord, who has always welcomed walkers says, 'what a good idea to get the young ones out walking with their parents!' He places no restriction during the day on children, but likes to keep the premises free during the evening for those who wish to dine. The delightful restaurant is very popular locally. There is a considerable choice of bar food and the menu is an interesting one.

Telephone: 0903 674 240.

How to get there: Hammerpot lies just north of the A27(T), opposite the B2225 road junction to Angmering village and is between Worthing and Arundel.

Parking: Providing that the landlord has been approached for permission to do so, his car park may be used.

Length of the walk: 4 miles. Maps: OS Landranger 197, Pathfinder TQ 00/10 (inn GR 067057).

This route is through woods, park and farmland, largely owned by Angmering Park Estates whose interests extend to horse and cattle breeding. On this walk you will pass by the paddocks and horse pastures for the mares and foals of the stud farm and will, no doubt, see the Highland cattle which are bred here – great shaggy gentle beasts with enormous horn spreads. The going is easy, all over gently undulating countryside. The woods are especially beautiful in springtime, being thickly carpeted with bluebells. There are some fine views to the south, looking out over the Channel.

The Walk

Leave the area of the pub to walk out to the junction with the A27(T) and turn right (west to Arundel) on the paved footpath. In only a few yards, turn right over a stile at a way sign going into a meadow. Keep the trees and hedge on the left and walk on towards the woods of Butlers Copse. Just before the woods, bear left on to a rough farm track and you will be approaching a bungalow. With this building and a two-way sign on the left, turn right on to a driveway. In the short distance to the next way sign, there are some magnificent chestnut trees. Here, at the two-way sign, turn left over a stile into a woodland path.

This path will continue on, with the car park at the Dover appearing on the left. At a way sign, go out on the lane and walk across it into a wide gravel track. Go by a two way sign on the right. The stony track will continue towards a flint-built house ahead – Dover Cottage. The field on the left usually contains a herd of Highland cattle.

With a two-way sign on the left, bear right (still on the track). At the next four-way sign on the left, the entrance into Wepham Woods, walk on. This will bring you to Wepham Call and Angmering Park Cottages on the right. With a three-way sign on

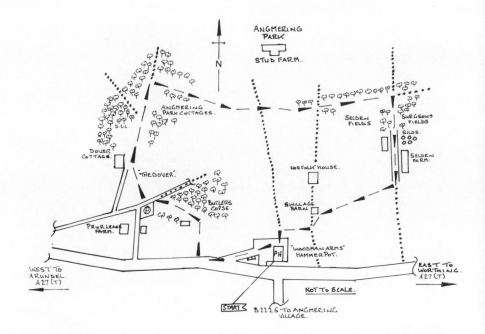

the left, turn right into the path going up by the building on the right.

With a two-way sign on the right, continue to the next two-way sign on your left and turn right. As you approach a third way sign, the path comes out of the woods and will now go between the paddock fences of Angmering Park Stud. As you come to the driveway of that establishment, bear right on to it and almost immediately left at a two-way sign and into a field path, with trees on the left. Coming to a gate, stile and four-way sign (all on the left), walk straight ahead – still on the field path. A beech hedge and paddock fence will be on the left. Continue on and the field path will pass more trees on the left. The path goes into the woods. At a farm track with a four-way sign, walk ahead on to another track which will continue through the woods of Selden Fields.

At the next four-way sign, turn right. Now on a track still going through woods, continue on to Selden Farm. With the old concrete silos on the left, continue past the converted farm buildings (also on the left) and, just beyond the last building,

94

Highland bull, Hammerpot.

turn right at a way sign onto a field path between fences. At the end of the path, go through a short section of trees and, at the other side (by a two-way sign), walk across a field to a house. Climb a stile with a two-way sign and on your right will be a house, Swillage Barn. Continue out on to the driveway to Norfolk House and at a three-way sign, turn left on to the drive.

With a pond on the left, turn right at a two-way sign into a field path. As you walk across this field the thatched roof of the Woodman Arms will come into view to your left. Go over a stile in the hedge, then a plank bridge. At the three-way sign turn left and very shortly you will be in the pub's parking area.

⓲ Findon
The Village House Hotel

The building was constructed in 1527, specifically as a coaching house, and during its existence has played many roles, notably as a magistrates' court where the unforgiving justice of the day was dispensed. The unlucky ones did not have far to go as the gallows were sited on what is now the village green (as the notice there testifies). Like all such places on main thoroughfares, 'Findon attracted all manner of thieves, footpads, highwaymen and other sundry vagabonds' as John Lower informs us in his *History of Sussex*. The old building has been extensively modified to fit its modern requirement, but its character remains. The main room is reminiscent of an eating establishment in earlier times and so are the gargantuan meals. All of the ingredients are fresh produce. There is accommodation for young children and a very pretty garden. Walkers are always welcome here with the proprietors, Ernest and Jean Brown.

On the second Saturday in September, the annual Findon Sheep Fair is held. This event is hundreds of years old and well

worth noting in your diary. Findon's other claim to fame is the horse-racing stables, most famous of which are those of Josh Gifford, the well-known trainer. It is a grand and not unusual sight to see the horses out on the gallops.
Telephone: 0903 873350 or 873521.

How to get there: Findon lies east off the A24, Worthing to London trunk road, and is approximately 4 miles north of Worthing itself. Leave the A24 at the main roundabout into the village. On reaching the crossroads at the village street, the Village House Hotel is on the left, with the Gun Inn opposite.

Parking: The car park specific to the Village House Hotel is very small and although the proprietors would be happy for customers to use it while they walk there is adequate on-street parking in the village and at the green close by.

Length of the walk: 3 miles or 3¾ miles if you go to the top of Cissbury Ring. Maps: OS Landranger 198, Pathfinder TQ 00/10 and TQ 01/11 (inn GR 122088).

This walk, in the heart of the downland, is not itself over hilly terrain. The route is all via bridleways, two of which can be very muddy after wet weather, bearing in mind the number of horses using paths in this area – alternatives are offered. You may be tempted with a diversion to the top of Cissbury Ring. Believe me, it really isn't as daunting as it may look – and once at the top, you can then walk around the ramparts of this neolithic fort. The views from here, as elsewhere on this walk, are magnificent. In summer, as with most other downland areas, there is a large population of skylarks filling the air with their lovely song.

You must appreciate that this is a very sensitive area into which to take dogs. Having said this, there is no reason not to, providing that when you are near to horses, your pet is properly leashed.

The Walk

With the frontage of the Village House Hotel on your right, walk the short distance back to the village crossroads and turn left. Within the space of a few yards, the village green will be on your left. Still on the left, pass the entrance of Stable Lane and walk straight ahead, past shops on either side, one of which, on

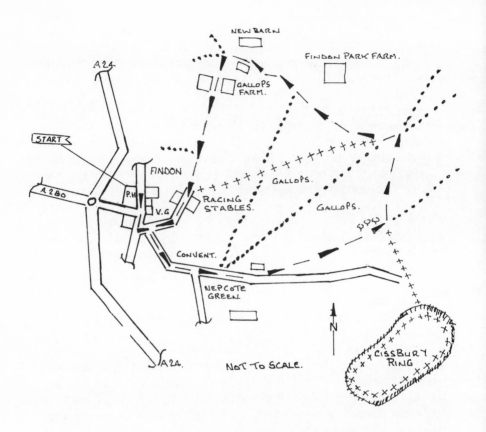

the left, is called The Green Wellie Tea and Coffee Shop. Walk
into Nepcote Lane, passing Summer Fields, then with Shrub-
lands on the left, the lane continues, going by a way sign on the
left. The lane soon forks. Take the left-hand one, signposted
'Cissbury Ring'.

Nepcote Green will now be on your right. You will see
Cissbury Ring rising beyond it. With a two-way sign now on the
right, walk straight on, passing Thistledown (a house on the
right), and then Ringhouse on the left. Turn left at a way sign
off the paved lane, into a narrow bridle track. The views across
to Cissbury Ring will open up, whilst on the left the Downs
training gallops will be below you and will remain in full view
for the whole of the length of this track. At the top end you go
through a small area of trees and emerge onto a wide crossing

98

track at a four-way sign (bridleways). From this point, you can appreciate just how close the foot of Cissbury Hill is along the track to your right. I've already said it is not as daunting as it may first appear – why not make the diversion?

Having reached the foot of the hill, it is clearly signposted to the top. After completing the circular walk around the ramparts, simply return down. From the top of Cissbury you will be able to see its neighbour, Chanctonbury Ring, to the north. Both these neolithic forts were subsequently used by the Romans.

Returning back to the four-way sign, either turn left (if you have not made the diversion) or walk straight ahead (wasn't that worth the effort?) and now, if the weather has been wet, you will be faced by mud, but, as you will see, walkers before you will have created some ways around it. Even from this level the views will expand all around as you progress along the way. Then, approaching the next four-way sign, turn left into another wide bridle track, which continues between paddock fences. The training gallops are still on your left.

Arriving at a three-way sign you can (if the weather has been wet and you have children with you) walk straight on down the stony bridle track. At the junction with the lane to Gallops Farm, signposted at the bottom going to the right, you turn left and continue from the final paragraph.

If using the other path from the three-way sign, turn right into the other bridleway. Paddock fences will be on your left and bramble thickets on the right. As you proceed you will see below you, to the right, Findon Park Farm and Findon Park House. At the next three-way sign, at a fork, walk into the right-hand branch. The track then continues for some way and a white-painted house will appear to your left on rising ground. Very shortly, the track will take you by the entrance way of New Cottage. The buildings of New Barn Farm are below you on your right.

With a gateway and four-way sign on your right, turn left into a rising stony track. Very shortly, you will be among the buildings of Gallops Farm. You simply walk out on to its concrete driveway, which you will see stretching out before you. Walk along its length and you will then be at the short-cut point.

Here at the three-way sign, with Josh Gifford's house and

stables establishment on the left, continue straight ahead into the lane (this is the top end of Stable Lane). Then, at a junction on the left, with a footpath sign, continue on down the lane. You are now, of course, in the outskirts of Findon. Still going downhill, passing Pony Farm and High Paddock, then with Kilmore Close on the right, the lane will emerge at the village green. Here you will be able to orientate yourself to your motor car and, no doubt, are more than ready for the delights of the Village House Hotel.

19 Thakeham
The White Lion

Built as a pub around 1640, this handsome house was one of a chain of distribution points operated by the infamous Hawkhurst Smuggling Gang, whose activity spanned from Hawkhurst in Kent to Ladyholt (Chalton) in Hampshire. The White Lion acted as the distribution centre for this area and was unique in that five tunnels terminated beneath the building, all starting from some distance away, thus, allowing the secret transportation of illicit goods well away from prying eyes. The present owner has charted the whole labyrinth and hopes to excavate some or all of the several miles of tunnels. The house has a benevolent green-cloaked ghost which the landlord has felt the presence of, but which other people have seen! It is also thought that the White Lion was used as a meeting place in the 17th century by William Penn, founder of Pennsylvania, whose family lived at Warminghurst, and his co-Quakers.

You can be assured of a warm welcome at this pub from owners, Bill and Patricia Newton. Patricia specialises in home

cooked food. With the exception of an addition some years ago, the old place is much as it was. In fact, the tiny village is also much as it was. Just to the west of the pub is a traditional Sussex timber-boarded cottage, sadly one of only a very few remaining in the county. The pub has a very large garden and the owners will provide children's meals at a reduced price. Barbecues are held regularly in the summer.
Telephone: 0798 813141

How to get there: Thakeham is just off the B2139, approximately 3 miles north of Storrington. Alternatively, it can be reached by taking the B2133 off the A24 at Ashington and then turning down Grays Lane.

Parking: Permission to leave your car in the pub's space while you walk will be readily given to customers.

Length of the walk: 3 miles. Maps: OS Landranger 198, Pathfinder TQ 01/11 (inn GR 108173).

At first sight one could be forgiven for believing that this tiny village is simply a collection of dwellings in a cul-de-sac. It actually contains several of the most picturesque old houses and cottages in West Sussex, some of which you will pass by at both the start and finish of this walk. The route takes you through three farms and over weald farmland. There are also some delightful woodland tracks. Most of this lovely walk is on good, firm tracks with no hills.

The Walk
Leaving the pub car park, turn right onto the lane passing the front of the building. Shortly, on the left, will be the entrance to Grays Lane from where you will see the parish church of St Mary. This ancient and beautiful building really merits a visit. Should you do so, there will be the added surprise of being able to see a few of the delightful old cottages close by the church.
Returning to the village lane, turn left through a gateway which leads to Thakeham Place Farm, whose buildings you will already have in view. Going over a cattle grid at a gateway, turn left, almost immediately going through a timber gate at a four-way sign. This takes you into a pasture, with some buildings of the farm on your right. A hedge will be on your left, whilst the

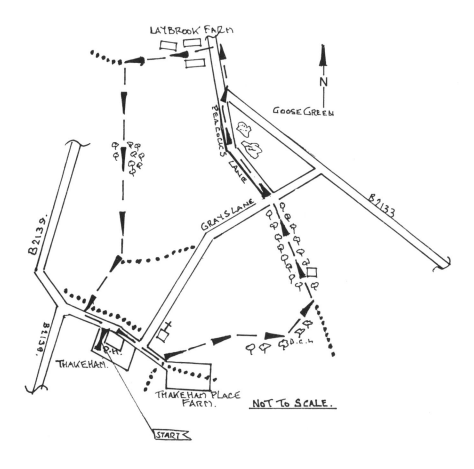

clearly defined path will top a rise and bring you to a stile, gate and two-way sign which gives access into the next field. The hedge is still on the left.

As you near the end of this field, a hunt gate will be on the left and a metal gate in front of you. Now turn right and in a few yards go through another gate at a two-way sign. You will be crossing over a stream – one of a number originating from St Mary's Well close by. The clearly defined path in this field is heading for the woods of Mill Copse. There will be a number of large, mature oak trees close by on your right, beyond which you will enter the wood through a gateway. This delightful woodland track, rising gently, will eventually bear to the left at the top of the wood where you will go over a stile at a two-way sign into a field.

There is an embankment topped by a fence on your right. Also on your right you will pass a line of mature oak trees. Look to your left whilst on this path for some wonderful views across the Weald. You will be able to see the North Downs in Surrey and unmistakable among those will be the 1,000 ft high Leith Hill.

Coming to the top of the rising ground in this field, the path drops down to a way sign, gate and stile giving access to a wide cart track. Once on this, turn left. I like to think (and believe) that this was one of the thoroughfares used by the smuggling fraternity in their active periods from the 17th century up until the early part of the 19th century. This track can be very muddy after rain. However, like most muddy spots in other areas, walkers before you will have made diversionary paths. You will pass, on the right, the ruins of New Barn and its stockyard. The track will eventually emerge on to Grays Lane. Cross over and continue into Peacocks Lane. It is advisable to walk on the right-hand side here to face the oncoming traffic.

At about halfway along the lane, you will pass by, on the right, a series of large ponds – old clay pits – then, on the same side, a large timber yard and sawmill. With a large brick house on the left, you are at the junction with the B2133 road. From this point and looking left, you will see your next way sign landmark. I would advise, despite the short distance, that you cross over to the other side of the road to take advantage of the wide grass verge there. Once opposite the way sign, cross the road again and walk into the paved track leading to Laybrook Farm (an Arabian Stud). As you approach the buildings, the farmhouse with a gate will be on your left. Bear right, still on the concrete paving, to continue between two buildings, and just beyond them turn right. Go through a gateway and facing you will be a timber-constructed bungalow, beyond which is a hedge with a wicket gate set into it. Go through this gate and turn left into the field. The hedge will be on your left and there, somewhat misplaced, is the way sign. The field path will continue alongside the hedge and deep cut stream on the left. Then, going through a metal gate into another field, the path continues to a second gate at a three-way sign. Once through

A traditional Sussex timber clad house.

the gate, turn left, negotiating a stile and footbridge.

There will be a timber power line support pole and hedge on the left, whilst on the right is an extensive area of orchards and vineyard. Walk straight ahead on a wide grassy track. Coming to a pair of twin power line support poles, you will be approaching a wood. With a two-way sign on the left, bear left through a line of oak trees. Bear right again and follow the direction of the way sign, into the woodland track on gently rising ground. You will come to a fairly unusual gate comprising three poles which can be released to gain access into the field in front of you. Please ensure these poles are replaced and secured after you. There is a two-way sign on the right and the path, bearing a little to the left, heads out across the field. Go towards the power line pole, one of two in this field, which is nearest to your left. When you come abreast of this, veer to the right, which takes you to a hedge in front of you. There you will see a two-way sign and, just beyond it, go through a steel gate.

You will now be on a wide track, heading towards a brick built red roofed barn. When you reach it, turn right over the stile at a three-way sign. This will put you on to a sandy track.

Continue on this and, where it bends sharply to the left (going to Thakeham church), walk off the track to go into Thakeham village sports field. Keep the hedge on your left and walk to the end of the field, from where, taking a flight of steps with a handrail, you descend on to the village street with the White Lion only a few yards away to your left.

Rowhook
The Chequers

'Chequers' is an immediate indication that this, or any other pub with the same name, is very old, as it will have had as neighbours, when first built, members of the Sorbus family of tree, for example the rowan and wild service, which have a collective countryside name – chequer tree. In the Autumn these produce a bright red berry which hangs on stalks in clusters, rather like cherries. This fruit would have been gathered, dried and offered to the customer. With the passage of time, the name became pluralised and chequers (draughts) boards appeared on the pub signs. This is the case at Rowhook and we can only suppose this was an easier explanation to make to the curious inquiring about the origins of the name.

The pub was purpose built in the 1400s and started life as the Chequer and, of course, has over the years been substantially modified. The old flagstone floor in the main bar has survived, as have many other original features, which gives it an air of welcome and warmth. There are extensive gardens and a family room, and the licensee, Tony Fulcher, and his wife, are very keen to encourage families and walkers. The menu is extensive and is produced from fresh ingredients and cooked the same day.

Telephone: 0403 790480.

How to get there: Rowhook lies north-west of Horsham and is reached on an unlisted road signposted from the A29 (Bognor road), just north of its junction with the A281.

Parking: There are two large car parks at this pub and the landlord is happy for walkers to use either, providing his permission is sought and his pub patronised.

Length of the walk: 3¾ miles. Maps: OS Landranger 187, Pathfinder TQ 03/13 (inn GR 112342).

The hamlet of Rowhook is bisected by Stane Street, the Roman road between Chichester (Nova Magnus) and London (Londinium). (My wife and myself, with our companions in 'The Sussex Wayfarers', have walked many sections of this ancient way, although this was a first for us.) You will leave the pub by walking first into Stane Street and then away from it on a bridle track which goes through 'Roman Woods'! Beyond this, and at the first of three farms, you will be on the Sussex Border Path, leaving it at the third farm to walk south, then back to Rowhook on the field paths.

The bridleway through Roman Woods can be muddy in winter, but the rest of the walk is over beautiful Sussex Weald countryside, with good views of the Surrey hills to the north and the South Downs, making this a delightful walk across gently undulating terrain.

The Walk

From the Chequers car park walk out onto the village street, bearing immediately right into the lane, Stane Street, with the pub and its garden then being on your right. Then, with Stane Cottage also on your right, continue on the lane to reach a notice direction sign 'To Waterland' and, with a way sign on the left, turn right, going through a gateway, and you will be facing a white painted half-timbered house. With a three-way sign on your right, continue straight ahead on a broad bridleway into the woods of Farthing Field. This clearly discernible track will

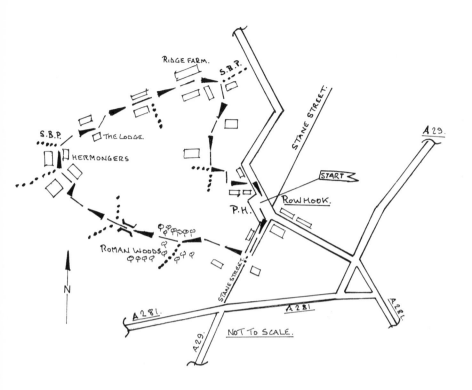

continue for some considerable way. Should it be muddy, the
secondary paths created by other walkers on either side of the
main track will be available to you. Then, with a three-way sign
on the left, bear right into the continuing bridle track now going
through Roman Woods.

Eventually, the bridleway will bring you to a two-way sign on
your right and here you will cross over a wide track and the way
will continue into the opposite woods. As the way begins to
descend it will suddenly reveal a two-way sign on your right.
From this point you will see an old brick-built bridge below
you. The way down is quite steep and you will need to watch
your footing. Having crossed over the bridge, walk on up to the
metal gate which you will see at the top of the rising ground.
There, with a three-way sign on the left, walk on beyond the
gate into the open field, keeping the fence on your right. This
field path will lead straight ahead to the buildings of
Hermongers and the farm of that name. Then, at the top of the

Rowhook hamlet.

field, with a three-way sign on the right, go through the gateway to turn right on to the metalled farm track, with the old farmhouse on your left.

The track will continue on and, coming to open ground on your left, you will see beyond it the imposing old buildings of Hermongers Manor. Continue, with farm buildings on either hand and with a modern white painted bungalow on the right. Just beyond this, at a three-way sign (also on your right), walk straight ahead into the eastbound Sussex Border Path. This metalled lane will bring you very shortly to The Lodge, a white painted building on the right. As you pass its massive old gate posts, turn right immediately beyond them at the three-way sign – you are still on the Sussex Border Path. Climb a stile which will take you by the north aspect of The Lodge and its garden (on your right) and where, just beyond and again on the right, you will pass large deer enclosures.

This field path will take you down to another paved farm track, coming from Hermongers Farm. At the two-way sign on the left, turn left and continue on the paved track which will take you by the end of the fenced area. You will pass by the buildings over to your right of Bury St Austens. The Surrey hills will loom large to your left, the unmistakable bulk of Leith Hill among them.

Next to come into view are the buildings of Bury St Austens Farm and, with a way sign on the left, walk across the trackway into the continuing Sussex Border Path, which will take you immediately through the barn yard, leading on beyond the buildings. The track is still paved and you will come to Ridge Farm, the third on this route. The track, as with the two previous farms, goes through the yards. Continue to a three-way sign on the left.

Here you would normally turn right, but when we did this walk we found the right of way had been obstructed by a big deer enclosure. If the obstruction is still in place, you will have to turn around and turn left at the opening leading down between two farm buildings and bear left around the building then on your left; in only a few yards, this will bring you to the other side of the obstructing enclosure. Bearing right here will put you back onto the correct path line.

With a fence on the left, continue down the field path, which, at the bottom of the field, will go over a stream to carry on into the next field. The wide, grassy track will be heading towards a gap in the tall hedge in front. Going through the gap and with a pond on the left, bear left onto a field path, with a fence and wood also on your left and large field on your right.

In only a short distance and coming to a two-way sign on the left, go over the stile there and turn right into a narrow, enclosed path. On the left is a timber fence, beyond which is a large house – Old Ockleys. As you approach a two-way sign on the right, the path branches right into a wider track, which goes between hedges. Before long, other buildings will appear between trees ahead. Pass by gates to the left and right. With a large barn on the right, other buildings are also on the left as you continue to a metalled track where you bear right at a two-way sign. Millfield House and farm are over to the right.

Carry on down this lane and, where it bends sharply right, walk across to the two-way sign, going over the stile there into a field. The field path continues and you walk the length of the field, keeping the hedge on the left. At the end of this field turn left at the four-way sign, which will quickly bring you to a two-way sign.

Turn right and walk down to yet another two-way sign. This will direct you to the left – a hedge and buildings will appear beyond it on your right. At the end of this field go over the stile. With a way sign on the roadside, turn right on to the road. In only a few yards you will pass, over on the left, the way sign leading into Stane Street, running alongside Rowhook Farm. You are, of course, back in Rowhook hamlet and only a short way from your starting point.